JAMES BOWIE

Texas Fighting Man

JAMES BOWIE

Texas Fighting Man

A BIOGRAPHY

CLIFFORD HOPEWELL

EAKIN PRESS Fort Worth, Texas
www.EakinPress.com

Library of Congress Cataloging-in-Publication Data
Hopewell, Clifford, 1914–
    James Bowie: Texas fighting man / by Clifford Hopewell. — 1st ed.
      p.   cm.
    Includes bibliographical references and index.

    1. Bowie, James, d. 1836.   2. Alamo (San Antonio, Tex.) — History — Siege, 1836.   3. Pioneers — Texas — Biography.   4. Texas — Biography.
I. Title.
F389.B8H66   1993
976.4'03'092 — dc20
[B]   92-44639
                                                              CIP

This book is dedicated to
my parents,
Emily and Harry Hopewell.

Jacob Buzzard (left) and James Black, blacksmith of Washington (Hempstead County), Arkansas. Black is the reputed inventor of the Bowie knife. (Collection of Stanley Dee Pruitt, great-great-grandson of Black)

Contents

"By Hercules! The man was greater than Caesar or Cromwell—well—Nay, Nearly equal to Odin or Thor. The Texans ought to build him an Altar!"

— Thomas Carlyle,
English essayist and historian,
speaking of James Bowie

Preface

As a native-born Texan whose favorite subject in school was history, I have long been fascinated with the state's past. Of particular interest to me are the men who shaped the destiny of the state in the early nineteenth century, and who played such a vital part in wrenching it from Mexico and becoming an independent nation. Men such as Stephen F. Austin, Sam Houston, James Bowie, William Travis, James Bonham, James Fannin, Davy Crockett, Thomas J. Rusk, Mirabeau B. Lamar, and others. All were heroes, and there was even a villain in the person of the pompous Santa Anna. Although he was not a participant in the Texas Revolution, the charming scoundrel and pirate Jean Lafitte has also intrigued me.

Like many people, I have my heroes. My two favorite heroes of Texas history are Gen. Sam Houston and his good friend James Bowie. I have already written the story of Houston in another biography. This volume focuses on the complex Bowie, whose fame as the wielder of the Bowie knife is legion.

Bowie was far from a saint; however, with his leadership qualities he might have been one of Sir Francis Drake's captains, or a general under Napoleon or a leader in the American Revolution under Washington. As it was, his destiny led him to the Alamo, to death and to glory and a lasting shrine in the pantheon of Texas heroes.

In researching Bowie I found many gaps in his life. Constantly on the go, there are many periods of several years where nothing is known of his whereabouts or activities. And of the many stories about this man, one wonders what is fact, what is legend, and what is myth. Sometimes they all merge, making it difficult to assess the real man. Yet two things are abundantly clear. In the wielding of his Bowie knife, the man was a deadly fighting machine. And in his love life the fates were exceedingly unkind. Prior to his marriage with the lovely Ursula de Veramendi, he had had unhappy love affairs with several women. Then, when he found happiness in his marriage, a cholera epidemic wiped out his wife of less than three years, their two children (it is doubtful if he even saw his youngest child, a boy), and his wife's family. He was never the same man again.

Among some knife fanciers there are questions as to whether the Washington, Arkansas, blacksmith by the name of James Black invented the Bowie knife as we know it today, or whether he even made one later. After consulting historians and men knowledgeable about knives, I am convinced that Black made at least one Bowie knife. There is at present a knife, reputed to be the one Bowie used at the Alamo, in the possession of a gentleman in California. At this late date there is no proof that this instrument was ever in the possession of Bowie, but my research leads me to believe there is an excellent chance Bowie used that particular weapon in the defense of the Alamo.

Books, magazines, newspapers, courthouse records, and other material researched for this book are mentioned in the body of the work, the footnotes, and bibliography. Until previously unpublished material is gathered, I believe this book to be as accurate an account of the life of James Bowie as is possible. It goes without saying that any errors of fact are mine.

Acknowledgments

Many people have helped me on the research of this book, and I am grateful to them all.

Jeanette C. Phinney, Bernice Strong, and the staff of the Daughters of the Republic of Texas Library at the Alamo; Ralph Elder and staff of the Center for American History, University of Texas at Austin; and the staff of the Texas State Archives in Austin all showed every consideration in making their facilities available to me and providing me with information about the fascinating James Bowie. Charles J. Long, former curator of the Alamo, was very helpful.

Bill J. Hughes, dean of students at Texarkana Community College, and Jim Batson are both noted authorities and knife collectors. Both provided me with much information about the Bowie knife and James Black, who reputedly invented the knife as we know it today. Batson, in particular, furnished me from his files much valuble information about Colonel Bowie and his family, as well as the Battle of the Sandbar, and he and I spent many pleasant hours in San Antonio and Austin digging up information about the colorful Bowie. Robert L. Tarin, Jr., archivist of Bexar County, was of immeasurable help in tracking down old records pertaining to Bowie and the Veramendi family. William R. Williamson., another noted authority on knives, provided me with important information about the Bowie knife and James Black. John D. Stokes came through with facts about the knife currently owned by Bart Moore and allegedly used by Bowie at the Alamo.

Thanks to Edmund C. Bowie, descendant of the famous James Bowie, who provided information heretofore unreported about some of the women in Bowie's lovelife prior to his meeting Ursula de Veramendi. Both Don Montgomery, historian, and historical interpreter of the Old Washington Historic State Park, Washington, Arkansas, and Stanley Dee Pruitt, great-great-grandson of James Black, dug into their records and provided much valuable information about the private life of James Black. I was fortunate to be put in touch with Alan Chapman of New Zealand. Chapman, a fan of the famous Bowie, was a source of much information about Stephen Bowie and various land transactions made in conjunction with his famous brother.

I cannot express my gratitude to the Church of Jesus Christ of Latter-Day Saints. There has been some speculation as to whether Jim and Ursula Veramendi Bowie had children. Through the International Genealogical Index (IGI) of the Family History Library of the church, birthdates of the two Bowie children were provided.

To Butch Winter, who kindly read my manuscript and made so many, many valuable suggestions as to grammar and spelling, and to my editor, Melissa Locke Roberts, who did the same.

Last, but far from least, thanks to the genius who invented the computer, thereby making the writing and revision of a manuscript oh, so much easier.

Thank you, thank you, thank you all.

JAMES BOWIE
Texas Fighting Man

Prologue

It was chilly in the predawn darkness of March 6, 1836, as the various brigades of the Mexican army, commanded by the president of Mexico, Gen. Antonio López de Santa Anna, assembled on the open fields near the Alamo. For thirteen days the 188 defenders of that ancient fortress had been under siege.[1]

For some weeks the Alamo had been under the joint command of the fiery William Barret Travis and James Bowie, the famous knife fighter. But now the popular Bowie was lying on his cot, seriously ill. He turned over sole command to Travis.[2]

On the evening of March 5, Travis assembled his men in the courtyard of the venerable fort and told them they were doomed. He stated that their appeals for help had gone unanswered and they could expect no more men to join their meager force; that each man had the choice to try to escape, or to stay and fight with him to the end. Drawing his sword from his scabbard, he then drew a line in the dirt and asked those who were prepared to die with him to step across the line. Of all the men present, only one man refused to cross the line. He was Louis Moses Rose, a veteran of the Napoleonic wars. James Bowie, confined to his cot, asked that he be carried across.[3]

The moment of truth had arrived.

At 1:00 A.M. the Mexican columns started marching, silently advancing toward the San Antonio River, which they crossed two men abreast over some narrow wooden bridges. Then, when they had reached a point previously designated by Santa Anna, they came to a halt and kept their silence. Precisely at 4:00, as the regimental bands started playing the "Deguello," the ancient Moorish bugle call of death signifying "no quarter," the various columns of the attacking forces swung into their assault and the Mexican artillery ceased firing. *El Presidente* Santa Anna commanded the reserve contingent of 400 men, which was safely stationed across the river in San Antonio, several hundred yards south of the Alamo.

When the first columns of infantry, under the command of Santa Anna's brother-in-law, Gen. Martín Perfecto de Cos, deployed, they advanced with their bayonets drawn. At first the troops advanced steadily in the slight mist. Suddenly, the guns from the fort opened up on them at point-blank range, leaving a wide path of wounded and dead among the Mexicans. Many of the defending Texans owned "Kentucky" rifles, whose steel barrel was four feet long and rifled so as to give the bullet a spiral motion, causing it to take a straight course. Living on the frontier as they did, virtually all of the Texans were expert shots and extremely accurate with their weapons up to 300 yards. Those who did not possess a Kentucky rifle used shotguns and fired buckshot. These were deadly at close range. The Mexican infantry muskets, predominantly English flintlock rifles firing one-and-a-half-inch balls, and with smooth bores and no rifling, did little damage at long range.[4]

When the first of the advancing Mexicans reached the Alamo walls and tried to scale them with their ladders, they were wiped out by buckshot. Many of the others were pushed backwards on their ladders and fell on the upraised bayonets of their compatriots.

When Cos and his column reached their assigned objective, they were swept back by the shotguns and rifles of the Texans and the four small cannons behind the palisades, which extended diagonally outward from the chapel front to the guardhouse. The disorganized troops at first retreated. They were then rallied by Gen. Juan Valentin Amador and, with the sheer weight of numbers pushing from behind, finally went over the wall of the outworks. Santa Anna then ordered Col. Augustin Amat to take his reserves into action, and also ordered into battle his general staff and everyone at his side. He himself stayed safely on the far side of the San Antonio River.

The close fire of the defenders took a devastating toll on the attacking troops. Col. Francisco Duque, commanding a battalion in the second column of the Mexican army, was rushing with his men toward the north front of the Alamo and fell, mortally wounded. Gen. Manuel Fernandez Castrillon then took command of the column and entered the presidio through a breach that had been made several days before during the Mexican cannonade. The column under the command of Colonels Jose María y Romero and Juan Morales then scaled the western walls. With so many of the enemy inside the fortress, many Texans sought sanctuary in the chapel; others retreated into various rooms in some barracks and bolted the doors.

After scaling the walls, some of the troops of Romero and Morales opened the gates to the Alamo, through which came the remainder of Cos' column. The four Texan cannons at the palisades were captured and turned upon the front doors of the chapel. The Mexicans, in overwhelming numbers, battered down doors of the rooms the Texans had barricaded themselves in, and a terrible hand-to-hand fight began as the Texans defended themselves with knives and by using gun butts as clubs.

Suddenly, the doors to the baptistry in the chapel of the Alamo were forced open by some of the attacking troops. Lying on a cot, his once powerful frame now emaciated due to illness, was a man with a brace of pistols, one in each hand, and a knife by his side. As the attackers rushed toward him, firing at close range and bayonetting him, the man's pistols fired and his famous Bowie knife went into action. Before the last breath had expired from his body he had taken several Mexicans into death with him. The remaining Mexicans, furious, tossed the dead body onto a dozen bayonets before finally throwing it onto the floor.[5]

James Bowie, for whom the famous Bowie knife was named, and the most famous fighting man in Texas, had passed into the ranks of Texas immortals.

Bowie knife and sheath

CHAPTER 1

The Beginnings

The forebears of James Bowie, who was famous for many things other than the knife that bears his name, were from the highlands of Scotland and can be traced back to the famed Scot, Rob Roy, and his wife, née Helen McGregor.[1] Moving up into Northern Ireland, they eventually immigrated to America.

The progenitor of the family in America was John Bowie, Sr., who went to Maryland around 1705 or 1706 at the invitation of his uncle, John Smith, and settled on the Patuxend River, near the village of Nottingham, in what is now Prince George's County. He died in 1759.[2]

The original John had a son whom he named John, Jr., and who, upon the death of his first wife, married one Elizabeth Pottinger. They had three sons, all of whom were in America before the Revolution. Two of them settled in Maryland, although later one of them moved to Virginia. The other son, James, was born about 1739. He moved to Edgefield, South Carolina, married a Miss Mirabeau, and was the paternal grandfather of the subject of this biography.

Not much is known of the original James, except that he was the father of four sons and a daughter and died young. The first two sons, twins, were born around 1762 and named Rezin (pronounced "Reason") and Resa.[3] Then followed John David, and the last child, Martha.[4]

A common thread running through the Bowie family is that over the years various branches moved to many states, including

South Carolina, Virginia, Georgia, Pennsylvania, Kentucky, Louisiana, and even to Canada.[5] There is even a difference in the spelling of the name, as some branches spelled it "Buie."[6]

As a group, the Bowies were interested in public affairs — the Maryland branch producing one governor — and they were shrewd in business. A James Bowie, a member of the Virginia clan, operated a ferry at Fort Conway on the Rappahannock, and is said to have ferried George Washington many times. When he died his wife, Sarah, took over the business and operated it successfully for many years. Many Bowies were successful planters and farmers, and they were constantly dealing in land.

Both Rezin Bowie and his younger brother John served as soldiers in the American Revolution. John served as a captain in the Fifth Regiment, South Carolina troop of the Continental line, while Rezin served as a private under Brig. Gen. Francis Marion, the great guerrilla leader who was known as the "Swamp Fox" due to his skill in harassing the British. Walter Worthington Bowie, whose book *The Bowies and Their Kindred* was published in 1899, revealed something about Rezin's military service:

> (He) served when a mere boy in the Patriot Army as private soldier under General Marion. At the storming of Savannah he was wounded and taken prisoner. In warding off a blow directed at his head by a British officer his hand was nearly severed by the saber of an Englishman. While confined in Savannah his wounds were dressed by the patriot women of that city, among whom was Elve Ap-Catesby Jones, daughter of John Jones, a Welsh emigrant. Young Bowie lost his heart with his nurse and married her in 1782, when not twenty years of age.

Rezin Bowie may have been young in years, but he was an excellent picker when it came time to choosing a wife. Elve, as she was commonly called, was a woman of character, determination, courage and intelligence. She was sweet-tempered and had an active mind. Various accounts describe Rezin as being tall, of fine physique, red-haired, fearless, and a man of high principles and personal integrity.[7]

When the war with England was over, Rezin and his new bride settled in Georgia. On October 1, 1784, and January 3, 1785, he requested and received from the state grants of land which he farmed. While in Georgia, the Bowies became parents of the first six of their eventual ten children. Twin daughters,

Lavinia and Lavisia, were born in 1783 and died in infancy. David, who became a pious member of the Methodist church, would die at nineteen by drowning in the Mississippi River. Another son, John J., was born in 1785. Next came Sarah, born in 1787, to be followed by Mary in 1789. The remaining four children were Martha, born in 1791; Rezin Pleasant, born September 8, 1793; James, born in Logan County, Kentucky, April 10, 1796;[8] and Stephen, the last of the Bowie children, born in 1797.

Like many pioneers in those early days in America, Rezin Bowie had the constant urge to move on. Consequently, by 1787 he had sold his Georgia property and moved to Tennessee. There Rezin further exhibited his love for land and for land transactions. On November 10, 1793, he purchased 640 acres on Station Camp Creek, one mile west of the village of Gallatin, from James and George Winchester. Two months later he sold 287 of those acres to James Odom. No doubt he quickly disposed of the other acreage, as by now he was preparing to move once more, this time to Kentucky, and the family settled in Logan County.

County tax records show Bowie as the owner of three slaves and five horses as of April 10, 1794. Rezin prospered and increased his holdings, as on March 20, 1795, he was listed as having eight slaves, eleven horses, twenty-three head of cattle, and one stud horse. A year later, on April 1, 1796, he was shown as the owner of eight slaves, seven horses, eleven head of cattle, and one stud horse. By 1797 he had acquired 200 acres of land by the waters of Red River, as well as nine slaves and eleven horses.[9] Clearly he was prospering. As late as September 16, 1799, the tax rolls list Rezin with the same property he owned in 1797.

Once more the urge to move on struck Rezin and Elve. The following winter Rezin sold his land in Kentucky, his stock and non-removable property to Ralph Law, and the Bowies headed for Missouri.[10] Law is recorded as owning, in 1800, the land that was formerly entered in the name of "Reason Bowey."[11] For some reason, the Bowies must not have liked life in Missouri, as in 1802 they gathered their possessions and moved outside the United States, settling on the Bushley Bayou in the district of Rapides, Louisiana.[12] As President Thomas Jefferson had not as yet effected the Louisiana Purchase, Louisiana was still under Spanish rule.

Bushley Bayou is shown on early maps as being located in

Ocatahoola, part of which became Catahoula Parish. In 1809 the peripatetic family picked up stakes and moved to Bayou Teche. Finally, around 1812, they settled permanently in Opelousas Parish, where, according to John Bowie, the elder Rezin died in 1819.[13]

Walter Worthington Bowie offered an example of the courage and resourcefulness of James' father and mother:

> In those early days Louisiana was filled with turbulent characters, who, attracted by the possibilities of the new region, flocked there in great numbers. There was little semblance of law, and the strong right hand was often called upon to protect both life and property, but Rezin Bowie was equal to such emergencies, and the turbulent class soon learned he was not to be intimidated ... He was fond of hunting, and his rifle ball seldom missed its mark. His wife also was a woman of rugged character, and endowed with masculine courage. Raised in the rough school of border life, she was a fit partner for her sturdy spouse. Many stories are told of their struggles with their aggressive neighbors. On one occasion, Bowie was compelled to defend his property against a set of reckless squatters encamped near him. In the conflict which took place he killed one of his adversaries, and a few days later he was arrested by a sheriff and charged with manslaughter; he was confined in an insecure wooden structure used as the "calaboose," or jail, to await trial. Mrs. Bowie knowing the constable to be an enemy of her husband, suspected he would allow his prisoner to be foully dealt with. Mounting her horse, and accompanied by a Negro servant on another fleet animal, she rode to the jail and demanded admittance to her husband's room. She was allowed to enter, and in a few moments re-appeared at the door accompanied by Rezin Bowie, each with loaded pistols in their hands. While the jailer sought a place of safety, they mounted the horses in waiting and rode away. It is not recorded that he was again molested.[14]

The senior Bowies had finally settled in their nest. The area had great swamps and vast forests, and once the trees were felled and the land prepared for cultivation, the soil was extremely rich. Once more the Bowie family prospered.

CHAPTER 2

Early Days

I t was in those early Louisiana years that the Bowie boys received their education and grew to manhood. James was only six years of age when the family first settled on the Bushley Bayou, but he and his brothers pitched in and helped their parents in felling trees and clearing the ground to plant the crops. The slaves probably did most of the hardest manual labor, but the boys did their share as well.

John, who was seventeen when the family first moved to this part of the southwestern frontier, stated that he and his siblings were reared "... most in remote and wild regions, and consequently grew up with but little education, or other advantages besides those inherited by natural endowment, or acquired from parental instruction."[1] Elve was religious — James once remarked she was a Methodist — and instructed her brood in the Bible and in Christian principles. According to John, Elve was responsible for much of the information the children in the family possessed.[2]

It is not too clear as to how much formal education Rezin, Sr., or Elve had. William R. Williamson, a writer, has made an extensive search of old records in Tennessee and Louisiana and was able to locate various types of documents, but could never find any document actually signed by Rezin. A seal bearing the signature "Reason" was always used.[3] In the case of a document with the signature of Elve, an "X" was used. The story goes that the children were educated at home in the backwoods. For what formal education they had, was it the father or mother, or both, who gave them their education, or perhaps some wandering French tutor?

All of the children learned to read and write. Both James and his brother Rezin learned to speak, read, and write both Spanish and French fluently, perhaps due to the numerous Cajuns and Creoles who lived in Louisiana. An examination by the author reveals that James wrote his Spanish in a clear, legible hand, unwavering and with all the lines written as if on ruled paper. His knowledge of Spanish in particular came in very handy in later life.

The boys may have had little formal education, but they all were leaders and became astute businessmen. Rezin P. became rich at an early age, and at one time was the owner of three separate plantations — one in Arkansas, another in Mississippi, and a third in Louisiana.[4] John, too, owned a fine plantation near Helena, Arkansas, and another in Mississippi. James was in and out of various business ventures all his life and constantly dabbled in land, as had his father before him. At one time he was a partner with both his elder brothers in their Arkansas plantations, as well as with younger brother Stephen.

Rezin and John became successful politicians in addition to their business interests. Rezin was three times a member of the Louisiana legislature and filled other important positions in that state, while John became a member of the territorial legislature in Helena, Arkansas.

John J. Bowie was married three times, first to Nancy Scroggins in 1806. By Nancy he had daughters Mary, Nancy, Hattie and Matilda, and a son, Rezin. After Nancy died in 1816, John married Lucinda Stewart, whom he later divorced. In 1830 John was married for the third time. The lady he chose was one American Watkins Kirkland, a widow, by whom he had John J., Jr., Martha, and James. John lived until 1859 and died at his plantation in Chicot County, Arkansas.

Rezin, who was extremely close to James all their lives, married Margaret Frances Neville in St. Landry's Catholic Church in Opelousas, Louisiana, on September 15, 1814.[5] The marriage was recorded in Marriage Record Book No. 1, page 256, of the St. Landry Catholic Church, and Rezin signed the book as "James Rezin Bowie." The couple had five children, two of whom died in early childhood. There was a daughter, Martha Andrewella, who died in New Orleans at the age of twenty-one in 1853. Matilda Eleanor married Joseph H. Moore, and when she became a widow, lived in New Orleans with a son, John S. Moore. Elve

Anne, named for her grandmother, was married to Taylor Moore and died in 1872 in Claiborne County, Mississippi.

During the War of 1812, Rezin served as a private in Col. Colman Martin's company and took part in the Battle of New Orleans. In 1815 he was elected colonel of the Avoyelle Mounted Riflemen and was commissioned by Governor Isaac Johnson.

Rezin was well respected by all of those who knew him. William H. Sparkes, who knew the Bowies well and was a neighbor of Rezin's at the time of the fall of the Alamo, described him as "a man of unusual mental and cultural attainments."[6] He died at the age of forty-eight on January 17, 1841. Originally buried across the river from his plantation in Iberville Parish, his body was later moved to Port Gibson, Mississippi, and reburied.

Living on the southwestern frontier was an education in itself. All the sons of the senior Bowie learned how to use the pistol, rifle, and knife and how to care for those weapons, as a thorough knowledge of them was essential to survival. The weapons were used in the hunting and stalking of animals to provide food, and the knife came in handy in dressing both large and small game. The boys also learned how to fish, as that helped provide food for the large family. They learned that to successfully run a farm or plantation required hard work and a knowledge of how to plant, cultivate and harvest money crops such as sugar cane and cotton. (Cotton was king in the South and Southwest in those days.) They learned something of animal husbandry, as there were cattle, mules, and horses to be taken care of.

James loved all the outdoor sports, such as fishing, deer hunting, horse racing, and coon hunting. He hunted turkeys and bears and alligators, and his sense of adventure led him to at least once ride an alligator.

The backwater swamps of Mississippi and Louisiana were infested with alligators by the thousands in those early years. Frequently passengers traveling down the rivers and bayous of Louisiana would amuse themselves by shooting at the alligators, just as years later, when the railroads opened up the West, and passengers on trains would shoot at the numerous buffalo roaming the prairies.

The alligators were so numerous that often hunts were organized to deliberately reduce their numbers. The farmers and planters had to do this in self-defense, as the "gators" were constantly devouring their hogs, poultry, cattle, and dogs. One such hunt, held in 1839 in the vicinity of Bayou Chere Amie and Glassy Lake, lasted only two and a half days. In that short period of time the hunters bagged "657 of the largest kind, not waisting [*sic*] a bit of powder upon anyone unless he measured a good ten feet in length."[7]

Living in the bayous, James and his brothers were very familiar with those beasts, and they grew up hating them. They were constantly on the lookout for them, and would frequently see two bulls fighting for the favors of a female, and hear the jaws of the reptiles clap shut. James in particular hated them as he observed the onslaughts they made on the farm animals and pets, or spoiled the fishing as they either chased away or ate the fish. Adventuresome and fearless, he learned how to rope alligators. This was no mean feat in itself, and took some courage as he had to get close to the reptile. If he lost his footing, the fast reptiles would be on him in a flash. An Indian boy taught him how to turn an alligator on its back and hypnotize it by rubbing its stomach. With his fearlessness, it wasn't long before James rode one.

The trick was to jump on the reptile in shallow water and, with his knife in his teeth and his arms and legs wrapped around the creature, hang on for dear life as the gator tried to shake him off. At an opportune moment he would then plunge his knife into a vital spot.[8] It was an exceedingly dangerous sport, as the alligators were powerful creatures, sly and cunning, and would try every trick in their trade to throw off the unwelcome rider. It must have been a momentous thrill indeed when the creature would dive into deep water, then roll and twist and turn, trying to drown young Bowie. One snap of those powerful jaws could have torn off an arm or a leg.

In August of 1936 J. Frank Dobie, noted Texas historian, visited E. A. McIlhenny, of Avery Island, Louisiana. McIlhenney had written a book on alligators the previous year, in which he related many of his personal experiences. During their conversation Dobie asked him what he thought of the claim that Bowie, in his youth, had ridden alligators. "I don't see why he shouldn't have ridden them," was the reply. "I used to ride them. The trick was to get on one's back, at the same time grasping his upper jaw firmly while gouging thumbs into his eyes. He couldn't see to do much, and the leverage on his jaw would keep him from ducking under the water with the rider."[9]

Another sport James engaged in was arrow fishing for alligator gar. The gar is another fearsome creature, being one of the largest and fiercest of all freshwater fish. Growing to a length of twelve or fifteen feet, these fish resemble the common pike. Their jaws are shaped like the bill of a goose and are armed with triple rows of sharp teeth similar to those of the barracuda, and their heads resemble those of alligators. Fishing for the gar was great sport, but it was so dangerous and required such skill that it was too foolhardy for one boy or man to risk it; consequently, Bowie always had companions on those expeditions. Unfit for human consumption once captured, the gar would be dragged onto ground and left for the alligators to eat.

Wild steers roamed the area and the Bowie boys would hunt them. Probably ancestors of the Texas longhorns, the animals were large, agile, fast, and had rapier-like horns that made them dangerous opponents. Hunting them was another sport that took courage to engage in, but the Bowie brothers were equal to the task. Sometimes the boys would shoot them and finish them off with a knife. Other times, James would use a lasso, and once the steer was tripped and on the ground, he or one of his brothers would dash in and with his knife cut its throat. This was definitely no game for weaklings to engage in, but the meat of those wild steers was prized and was a familiar part of the diet of the Bowie household.

Not the least of the sports engaged in was that of hunting and trapping bears. According to his brother John,

> He [James] had a way of catching bears which was entirely original. In the summer season, when the bears were constantly ravaging the little patches of green corn of the early settlers, he adopted the following novel plan to entrap them. After finding the place where they usually entered the field, he procured a hollow *cypress knee* of suitable size, which was properly cleaned out, and then sharp iron spikes were driven through it with the points inward and inclined downward, similar to the fingers of a fish trap. Being thus prepared, some honey (of which the bear is passionately fond), was put in the bottom of the inverted knee, and this put at the place where the bear crossed the fence.

In his eagerness to get the honey, Bruin would thrust his muzzle
and head down amongst the spikes, and when he would attempt
to draw out his head, the spikes would pierce the skin and flesh
in such a manner as to prevent him from throwing off the *mask*,
and in this blindfolded condition he became an easy prey to his
gleeful captor.[10]

With the hard work he engaged in on his parents' plantation, in addition to living such a hardy outdoor life, James Bowie
grew into a magnificent physical specimen. The man was all
muscle, being 6'1, weighing 180 pounds, with broad shoulders.
His eyes were gray-blue, deep-set, and penetrating in their glance,
while his hair was chestnut brown. Although he was constantly
exposed to the sun, his complexion was fair. His hands were long,
slender, white, and very capable, and he had a steel-like grip.[11]

Although young and friendly with everyone, Bowie was ambitious and, said John, was always careful to form his friendships
and associations with only the best class of the backwoods community in which he lived.[12] He was fond of music and would take
a glass when in a merry mood, and he was courteous with all
women. But on occasion, related brother John, "his anger was
terrible and frequently terminated in some tragic scene."[13]

From early on, in any activity engaged in by James, he was
usually the leader. Noah Smithwick, who knew him well and some
years later fought with him in the Battle of Concepción, thought
highly of Bowie and described him as "by nature calculated to be
a commander of men."[14]

Although James, Rezin, and John were always very close and
often pursued business ventures together, James and Rezin were
extremely close all their lives. This might have been due to their
closeness in age, as between the two there was only two years'
difference, while there was a ten-year gap between James and
John, the eldest of the Bowie brothers.

According to Lucy Leigh Bowie, a relative of the Bowies,
James and Rezin were "partners in everything from their baby-
hood, and Rezin's marriage in 1812 to Margaret Frances Neville
. . . did not separate the brothers."[15]

In 1814, when he was eighteen, Bowie left home and settled
in Rapides Parish, Louisiana. A ledger dated 1817 records purchases he made at a general store, later Bennett's store, on Bayou
Boeuf, near the town of Cheneyville. He cleared a piece of land

and for several years supported himself mainly by sawing planks and lumber with a whipsaw, and boating it down the bayou for sale.

Sometime in 1818 or 1819, Rezin Bowie, Sr., started James and Rezin P. off together in life by giving them each ten servants, horses, and cattle.[16] The brothers were hard-working and intelligent, as well as ambitious, and they operated their plantation successfully. In the seven or eight years they operated in partnership, they owned and developed several valuable estates in the Lafourche and Opelousas parishes.

In 1825 the brothers, together with their youngest sibling, Stephen, sold the Bayou Boeuf plantation and purchased Acadia, their plantation near Alexandria, in Rapides Parish. They skillfully improved Acadia until it became celebrated far and wide as a model estate. During the grinding season of 1827, the brothers installed machinery and set up the first steam mill for grinding sugar cane in Louisiana. Until then, mule power had been used. It was to Acadia that James would bring his widowed mother to live.[17]

On February 12, 1831, in a transaction recorded in Lafourche Parish, James and Rezin — together with Stephen, who was their partner in various land purchases and sales — sold Acadia for $90,000 to R. J. Walker, D. S. Walker, and J. C. Wilkins. The purchase price also included sixty-five slaves.

James became co-owner with Rezin of a plantation in Arkansas, and John Henry Brown, who traveled with him on the Mississippi in 1829, stated that James also "owned a large plantation, called Sedalia, and negroes, near Natchez, on the west bank of the Mississippi."[18]

Although the brothers were making money with their plantation, it was not enough to satisfy their ambitions, and James' ambitions in particular. They cast around for other opportunities to make money and found one. It was in the sale of black ivory. To be specific, it was the smuggling and selling of slaves, and they dealt with Jean Lafitte.

CHAPTER 3

Lafitte the Pirate

Jean Lafitte had been a notorious pirate who, for his assistance in helping Gen. Andrew Jackson win the Battle of New Orleans in 1815, had been pardoned by President James Madison for all of his past crimes.

The brothers Lafitte, Jean and Pierre, first appeared in New Orleans sometime in 1806. They established a blacksmith shop on St. Philip Street and later a fine store which they operated on Royal Street. The brothers prospered, and entertained lavishly in their mansion at the corner of Bourbon and St. Philip streets, a few short squares from the courthouse and the Church of Saint Louis.[1]

The Lafittes were Frenchmen who had come to Louisiana by way of the West Indies, and were known to be agents for the smugglers of Barataria. They dealt in slaves, as well as fine merchandise, which they fenced through their store on Royal Street.

Jean, although the younger of the two brothers, was the leader of the pair. He had been born around 1780, while Pierre was two or three years older. Jean was some six feet tall, slim and well made, extraordinarily strong, and very handsome. Like many men of those days he was an expert with the foils, and it was rumored that he had once killed a man in a duel with the weapon. Although he seldom smiled, he was a man of great personal charm and was attractive to women. Exceptionally neat in his dress, his hair was sleek and black and sometimes he wore a mustache and affected sideburns. The two brothers were accepted by the businessmen of New Orleans, but were never asked to meet the wives and daughters of their business acquaintances.[2] Both of the men, as was common in that day and place, had quadroon mistresses and had illegitimate children by them.

Until 1810, Jean and Pierre had been content to act only as the city representatives of merchandise and slaves furnished by the pirates and smugglers operating out of Barataria, but the situation had changed. Until January 1, 1808, the importation of slaves into the United States was legal. On that date, however, a law went into effect prohibiting their importation, and throughout the South the price of the black ivory, as they were known, immediately rose. Slaves could be bought in Africa for $20, or for $300 in Cuba, which had become the headquarters of the illegal slave trade. Due to the shortage of merchandise, plantation owners were gladly paying from $800 to $1,000 for an able-bodied black man, and smuggling into Louisiana became immensely profitable.[3]

Jean Lafitte was a genius at organization. He learned that there was great dissension between the smugglers and pirates operating out of Grande Terre Isle in the Bay of Barataria, some sixty miles south of New Orleans. At the northern end of the bay a dozen bayous led into the swamps, and from this marine labyrinth smugglers had been operating almost continuously since the early days of French rule. Quarreling between the smugglers and pirates was so great that the two factions were almost at war with each other.

Lafitte appraised the situation and departed for Grande Terre after leaving the New Orleans business in the hands of Pierre. At Grande Terre, Lafitte found the colony a mixed one consisting of smugglers, a group who referred to themselves as privateers, and others who boasted that they were out-and-out pirates. In addition, there were several hundred assorted thugs, ruffians and riffraff, and some 200 women of similar character and dubius morals.

Within a few weeks Lafitte had conferred with all the leaders of the various factions. He pointed out that under his leadership and his facilities for disposing of slaves and merchandise, there would be greater profits for all. They listened, and they accepted his leadership. One of the rules he instituted was that every Baratarian ship must have letters of marque from a country at war with Spain, and that only Spanish vessels were to be attacked. Within a year he had more than 1,000 men under his command, and fifty ships were bringing their prizes into Barataria.

Lafitte was wise enough to keep the men he now controlled happy. Thatched cottages were built for the pirates and their women, and gambling houses, cafes and bordellos were opened so that not only the pirates but any visitors to the island could have their entertainment. Vast warehouses for the loot seized at sea were built, as well as slave quarters where the blacks taken from captured slavers were held in chains, awaiting to be inspected and purchased. Lafitte built himself a mansion of brick and stone in the center of the colony and equipped it with the finest of furniture, linens, plates and carpets — all stolen by his pirates.

In his luxurious surroundings Lafitte entertained his business friends from New Orleans, as well as the slave owners and the plantation owners who would bid on the black ivory at the frequent auctions. The slaves would then be smuggled into Louisiana.

In Louisiana, Pierre was selling the fine merchandise captured by the pirates and taking orders for more. By 1813, at the height of the Lafittes' popularity, so much smuggled merchandise was being supplied to the New Orleans merchants that the legitimate commerce of the city was beginning to suffer.[4]

Although Lafitte professed that he was only a privateer conducting operations solely against the Spanish, evidence slowly began accumulating that he was, in reality, a pirate. In 1813, he and his brother Pierre were charged with smuggling. The Baratarians had been growing more and more arrogant, and had been preying on British merchant ships. This caused the American authorities to start taking an interest in the activities of the Lafittes. On October 14, 1813, Walker Gilbert, an American revenue officer with a company of dragoons under his command, had caught Jean and his men with a shipload of contraband goods in the marshes near New Orleans. A skirmish ensued and Gilbert and his men succeeded in taking possession of the pirate schooner and its contents. The Baratarians attacked once more in fury, routed the soldiers, and recovered their illegal booty.

This action so disgusted William C. C. Claiborne, governor of Louisiana, that on November 24, 1813, he issued a proclamation offering a reward of $500 for the capture and deliverance of Jean Lafitte to the sheriff of the Parish of New Orleans. Two days later a similar proclamation appeared at the identical places where the governor's had been shown. This was a parody of Claiborne's proclamation with the names reversed. A reward of $1,500 was being offered for the arrest of William Charles Cole Claiborne, and for his delivery at Grande Terre. The proclamation was signed by Jean Lafitte.

Claiborne did not enjoy being made a fool of, and he attempted criminal proceedings against the Lafittes. The grand jury, in session, returned indictments against Jean and his brother and other Baratarians, and Pierre was arrested and placed in the calaboose without bail. Jean hired two of the ablest lawyers in New Orleans to defend his brother, for a fee of $20,000 each, and then went into hiding. For several months Pierre languished in jail, despite his attorney's best efforts to secure his release. Eventually, he was freed by a mysterious jailbreak.

In September 1814, England and the United States were at war. The British were occupying Washington, and ships of his Majesty's Royal Navy were approaching Louisiana. On the third of the month the British landed at Grande Terre; several officers were rowed ashore and requested an audience with Jean Lafitte. The audience was granted, a fabulous lunch was served, and after the meal cigars and wines were passed around.

The British officers then got down to business. They offered Lafitte $30,000 in gold and a captaincy in the British navy if he and his men would enlist in the British cause and help in the coming attack against New Orleans. The pirate chieftain listened courteously to their proposal, and asked for time to think the matter over.

After the British left, Lafitte promptly wrote Governor Claiborne of what had transpired. In his letter he offered the services of himself and his men to defend Louisiana, and "the only reward I ask is that a stop be put to the proscription against me and my adherents, by an act of oblivion for all that has been done hitherto."[5]

For some months Claiborne had been pressing the federal government to clean out Barataria. In a conference with the army and naval commanders to decide whether to accept Lafitte's offer, both Commodore Patterson of the navy and Colonel Ross of the army voted in the negative, and Lafitte received no answer to his proposal.

Commodore Patterson began assembling his forces for an assault on Barataria. On the morning of September 11, 1814, Patterson's force left New Orleans, to be shortly joined by six gunboats and the schooner *Carolina* under the command of Colonel Ross. The fleet sailed slowly along the Gulf Coast, and early in the morning of September 16, Grande Terre and Grande Isle were in sight. When the fleet was first sighted the Baratarians prepared to resist the invasion, as they thought it was the British returning to attack them.

To the surprise of the pirates, the American flag was unfurled. Not willing to fire on that flag, the men put up no resistance but fled in every direction, abandoning everything. Many hundreds escaped in the numerous marshes, but even so, eighty men were captured. The Lafitte brothers managed to escape, but Dominique You, their number-one lieutenant, was among those captured. When the soldiers under the command of Patterson and Ross broke into the vast warehouses and seized the rich merchandise stored there, they valued their prize at more than $500,000.

In addition to the captured merchandise, Commodore Patterson's official report stated: "I have brought with me six fine schooners, and one felucca, cruisers, and prizes of the pirates, and one armed schooner under Carthagenian colours, found in company and ready to oppose the force under my command."[6]

The pirate stronghold of Barataria was no more.

When Jean Lafitte reached New Orleans, he called upon the governor and renewed his offer to serve with the Americans. Claiborne referred the matter to Gen. Andrew Jackson, who was then at Mobile, Alabama, on his way to New Orleans. Jackson rejected it with scorn.

Jackson reached New Orleans on December 2, 1814. When he made an inspection of the city's weak defenses and the small number of regular troops and militia at his disposal, he was appalled. Especially so as his information told him the British had 12,000 troops heading for New Orleans.

Lafitte promptly took advantage of the situation and called upon the general in person, once more offering his services as well as those of his men. This time Jackson gladly accepted the offer, together with the 7,500 pistol flints which Lafitte had had hidden in secret storehouses in the swamps.

Jackson, who by now had declared the city under martial law, promptly ordered all of Lafitte's men released from jail. Together with the two brothers, they were then mustered into the American army.

The Battle of New Orleans commenced on December 23, 1814, when Jackson, who was a fighting general, ordered his troops to attack on the plains of Chalmette before the British had effected their disembarkation. The decisive battle did not occur until January 8, 1815, but while the battles were raging Lafitte and his men, especially the experienced artilleryman Dominique You, rendered invaluable assistance. On February 6, 1815, Lafitte received his reward. On that date President Madison issued a proclamation giving a full pardon to the pirate and his Baratarians. The Battle of New Orleans had been a useless one, as peace between the United States and Great Britain had already been signed before the first shot was fired.

After the war was over, and although he and his men had been pardoned by the president, Lafitte was a restless man. He sensed that his popularity had declined in New Orleans. He knew that his stronghold in Barataria was now unsafe for any smuggling or privateering operations, so he decided to seek another base for his operations.

Gathering Pierre and a number of his men with him, including the redoubtable Dominique You, Lafitte outfitted some vessels and headed for Port au Prince in the West Indies. The group quickly found out that they were not welcome, so for some time the pirate leader and his men sailed the Gulf of Mexico looking for a suitable home. Finally, sometime in 1816, he founded a small colony on an island off the coast of Texas and called it Campeachy, under the impression that it was in the bay of that name.

When Lafitte learned of his mistake, he changed the name to Galvez-town, which eventually became Galveston.[7] He began to fortify the island and effect a permanent settlement, and once news of his new establishment spread, followers rapidly flocked back to him. For his home, Lafitte built a new dwelling that was a combination of residence and fort. The building was strongly constructed, with cannon visible through apertures in the upper story, and was painted bright red. He named it Maison Rouge.

Once more Lafitte started engaging in his smuggling and privateering, if not downright piracy, activities.

CHAPTER 4

Dealer in Black Ivory and Land

T he smuggling and selling of slaves was indeed a very profitable business, and James and his brothers were never averse to making a dollar. James was young, ambitious, and wanted to make money. Due to his logging operations, and later on with his operation of the sugar mill, he had visited New Orleans numerous times. Although successful in his business, he was still a very young man who had lived in the backwoods and swamps all of his life.

Bowie was impressed with the social climate of the Paris of the West, and had met and done business with successful businessmen and dandies residing in that city. He noticed their manners, their customs, and their dress, and realized that with his lack of formal education he was not in their social class. Yet he knew he already had several advantages that were in his favor: He was very social, had immense personal charm, made friends very easily, and people gravitated to him. More money would help him acquire the needed social polish to be the equal of the men he dealt with frequently.

The population of Louisiana was increasing rapidly as newcomers were arriving almost daily; consequently, land values were increasing rapidly. Bowie, with his intelligence, saw the vast profits that could be made in land speculation. But to speculate meant that one had to have sufficient capital, and that was something the Bowies did not have. The slave trade offered that opportunity since it did not require as much money to get started. Besides, it had other advantages in that the profits were both quick and large.

To finance his new venture, James sold his land on the bayou, and he and Rezin sold their sawmill. Brother John joined them in their new project.

According to the *Galveston Daily News,* March 16, 1920, a gentleman by the name of Warren D. C. Hall knew Jean Lafitte, and on a trip to Rapides Parish met James Bowie and apprised him of the opportunities to be had in the smuggling of slaves should he visit Campeachy. Early in 1818, James and Rezin accepted Hall's invitation to visit the pirate, and were accorded a royal welcome by the buccaneers. Lafitte took a great liking to James, who returned the affection. The two men had much in common since they were both personable, fearless, charming, imaginative, and adventurous. It was said that they even looked alike. Lafitte was an inch taller, but in a physical way they resembled each other remarkably.[1]

The two men quickly came to terms on their business arrangement, and it was agreed that James would pick up the slaves at the Lafitte stockade on Campeachy. It was no easy task to import the slaves from Galveston into Louisiana, as they would have to travel several hundred miles through the swamps of East Texas and Louisiana.

The Bowie brothers had a good thing going, and they took advantage of it. Most of the southern states had laws that permitted any informer on smuggled slaves to receive half of what they brought at public auction. Thus, the Bowies would carry the slaves they purchased from Lafitte to a customhouse officer and inform on themselves. The United States marshal would then sell the blacks at auction; the Bowies would purchase them and receive back, as informers, half the price paid for them. They then had legal title to them and could sell them anywhere in the South.[2] The slaves were later transported to New Orleans and to various plantations in Louisiana, sometimes far up the Mississippi, where a prime individual would often bring in $1,000.[3]

Apparently it was James, accompanied by his faithful slave Sam, who actually did the slave running, as his brothers stayed home and took care of other businesses. According to Horace H. Shelton, Bowie made three trips to Galveston Island to purchase slaves from Lafitte.[4]

Although there was much money to be had in the running of slaves, the business was not without its risks. On a return trip from Galveston James went to sleep, leaving his faithful Sam with the task of guarding the merchandise. When Bowie awoke he discovered that Sam had fallen asleep on the job, and thirty slaves had disappeared. As that particular section of country abounded with the fierce and cannibalistic Karankawas, Bowie assumed the Indians were the raiders. He promptly gave hot pursuit, following the Indians west to the Colorado River in Texas, but never overtook the Karankawas or recovered his property.[5] The loss of slaves at an average purchase price of $140 represented a loss of $4,200, a considerable sum at the time.

Although today we look upon the dealing and trafficking of humans as reprehensible, at least James Bowie and his friend Lafitte were not without some scruples. It was the custom of many heartless slave dealers to take a slave who was ill, or in some way incapacitated (usually due to the brutality and starvation methods of the slaves while on shipboard), and knock him in the head and dispose of him. That was not the way Bowie and Lafitte operated. They would offer a smaller sum than the prevailing rate per pound, purchase the slave, and take care of him and feed him properly until he had fattened up. Then they would sell him for what the market would bear.

Elder brother John later left an account of the smuggling activities of the brothers: "James, Rezin and myself fitted out some small boats at the mouth of the Calcasieu, and went into the trade on shares. Our plan of operation was as follows: we first purchased forty negroes from Lafitte at the rate of one dollar per pound, or an average of $140 for each negro . . . we continued to follow this business until we made $65,000 . . . when we quit and soon spent all our earnings."[6]

Although it seems that James, alone among the brothers, actually did any slave running, on at least one occasion Rezin was involved in the business.

William H. Sparkes of Atlanta, Georgia, was purportedly an intimate of the Bowies. The following is his version of how Rezin, although not actually running slaves, acted on behalf of a friend to save him from taking a heavy loss as a result of confiscation of some of his slaves by the State of Georgia:

> About 1817 or 1818 there were imported into Georgia by certain parties a number of African Negroes. They were discovered and taken possession of by the State authorities and

brought to the seat of government, Milledgeville, and by some process of pretended law were sold into slavery to the number of fifty or sixty. These were carried away and retained by the purchasers when the sale was arrested. The remaining sixty or seventy were retained in custody of the officers of the State. There appeared a claimant by the name of Madraza from Havana, for these slaves. The slave trade then was legitimate in all the Spanish-American possessions. It was proven that John Madraza, of Havana, was the owner of the ship, and the slaves captured in Georgia were all that had been saved from the wreck, which had occurred on the coast of Florida; that they had been taken possession of by parties who had no interest in the ship or slaves, and secretly carried into Georgia.

The suit before the court was to recover the money for the slaves sold and those remaining in the hands of the State officers. Madraza appeared with an interpreter, as he could only speak Spanish. At the final trial, proof of the most unquestionable character was produced to establish the identity of Madraza, and that he was a resident merchant of Havana and the owner of the ship and cargo. A recovery was had of the money and the Negroes, all of which was paid and delivered to Madraza.

The prime mover and he who had furnished the money to buy and ship these Negroes resided in New Orleans. The Negroes were purchased in Cuba from a regular trader and shipped to Apalachicola, and sent up to the agency of the Creek Indians, where they were captured. The New Orleans owner knew Rezin P. Bowie, and to him communicated the condition of things and asked his aid. 'It is easy enough,' said Bowie, 'to establish a house in Havana, let it claim the Negroes, let the ship be lost, and the Negroes stolen and carried into Georgia, without the consent of the owners.' It was left to Bowie, who was to be amply compensated if successful. He established the house, was himself Madraza, furnished the proof and succeeded, but was never compensated.

It is not known exactly how long James engaged in the smuggling and selling of slaves — probably not more than two years — and he didn't engage in the business full time. He joined the Long expedition into Texas.

Dr. James Long, a surgeon from Mississippi, had served under Jackson in the Battle of New Orleans as a member of Gen. William Carroll's brigade. He decided to free Texas from the grip of Spain. In June of 1819, gathering some seventy-five followers, he marched into Texas with his small army and with little resistance captured the East Texas town of Nacogdoches. Long and other leaders then declared Texas to be a free and independent republic. It is known he had correspondence with Lafitte, and visited him at Maison Rouge in the summer of 1819. Perhaps Bowie met the doctor while visiting his friend the pirate, and decided to join that 1819 expedition. No one knows for sure, since virtually nothing is known of Bowie's participation in the affair. Long's invasion eventually collapsed and he later was assassinated in Mexico City.[7]

Eventually the United States government got tired of the depredations upon American citizens and the general piratical acts of Lafitte and his men. One day in early 1821, naval officer Lieutenant Kearny appeared at Campeachy in the United States brig-of-war *Enterprise*. He delivered a message to Lafitte that the pirate understood: Lafitte was commanded to abandon Galveston. The buccaneer realized the inevitable, and requested two months' time in which to arrange his affairs. The request was granted. During that period of time, Lafitte called his men together and passed on the demands of the government, stating that everyone must leave. He himself had determined to destroy Campeachy.

Sometime in March 1821, Lafitte burned Galveston, completely destroying the settlement while the sailors aboard the *Enterprise* watched the flames. Galveston was no more.

Now that James Bowie's slave-running days were over he became restless and was always on the move. John moved his various operations in Mississippi and Arkansas, and in the latter state he named his plantation "Bowie."

James never settled down permanently. He visited Natchez and Arkansas, went on long hunting trips, and then visited New York. In 1824 he went into Texas again, visiting San Antonio de Bexar on a trading venture. In New Orleans he spent much of his time renewing old friendships and creating new ones. He was popular wherever he went, and was accepted in society. He took in the Saturday parades in the Place d'Armes and the twice-weekly masked balls at the French theater. Undoubtedly he attended the numerous quadroon balls that were held to display the city's beauties for young dandies.[8]

While in New Orleans, Bowie had his portrait painted, and he became friendly with the actor Edwin Forrest, who was just beginning to make a name for himself on the American stage.

About 1826, James started speculating in land in Louisiana, selling titles to land grants. According to John, "James went into the land speculation and soon made $15,000 . . . this business necessarily caused him to spend much of his time in the woods, where natural inclination also gave the employment a charm peculiarly pleasant to him."[9]

This land speculation requires an explanation.

In 1803, when the United States purchased Louisiana, a promise was given that the rights of all settlers then in that vast area should be protected. The United States began an investigation in 1806 to determine who was entitled to preference in land claims. This investigation extended itself through more than twenty years, although it was fairly certain that all honest claims had been confirmed sometime before 1820.

From 1820 through 1824, Congress was overrun with claimants who contended they had been overlooked and thereby wronged. Congress, therefore, on May 26, 1824, authorized the superior courts of the various territories to try these new claims. Suddenly, the claims became entangled in lengthy and expensive litigation.

In the latter part of 1827, the Superior Court at Little Rock, Arkansas, was flooded with 126 claims for confirmation, all concerning lands located in Spanish grants sold by John J. or James Bowie, or some other land speculators, to men who lived in Arkansas. These purchasers were ignorant of the origin of the claims they were pressing for settlement. Most of the claims were for 400 arpents of land (less than 500 acres). Between December 19 and 24, 1827, the Superior Court confirmed 117 of those claims, and practically all of the claims of the Bowie brothers were among those confirmed.[10]

Noah Smithwick remarked in his *Evolution of a State*: ". . . the case was in all the courts and became celebrated as 'The Bowie Claim.' The Bowies won their suit, and had a fortune, but Jim was prodigal with his money, though he was no gambler, and soon let his share slip away from him . . . in the same way a fortune which he was said to have made out of the slave trade, carried on in connection with Lafitte, filtered through his fingers."[11] Within a few weeks of their victory, John Bowie had prepared twenty-four more grants of the same kind, and then "with other parties," thirty more, and sold them very rapidly. It is not known whether James was one of the "other parties."[12]

The land grant speculation trials did not stop with the 1827 Superior Court decision, since in Arkansas, United States District Attorney General Samuel C. Doane appealed the case. He suspected fraud, and asked for time to go deeper into the Spanish language, laws, and records.

The outcome of it all was that on February 7, 1831, the court reversed itself. Most of the claims were based on alleged grants to one Bernardo Sampeyreac by the Spanish governor of Louisiana in 1789. The court found that Sampeyreac was a fictitious name and that the grants were forgeries. It had clear proof that witnesses for the claimants in the first trial had been bribed, and that sales by the Bowies and various other speculators were fraudulent.

After one more appeal, in 1833 the Supreme Court of the United States confirmed the opinion of fraud and forgery. Not an acre of ground had actually been conveyed to any "innocent" purchasers from the Bowies and fellow speculators in Spanish grants.[13] By then, it didn't matter to James Bowie. He was among those who long ago had "G.T.T." — Gone To Texas.

CHAPTER 5

Battle of the Sandbar

For some time Bowie had been making Alexandria, Louisiana, on the Red River, his business headquarters. In 1826 he became involved in a street brawl that gained him a certain amount of notoriety and was the beginning of his fame as a fighting man.

James had participated in some political party squabbles of the day and had made some enemies, among whom was Maj. Norris Wright, reputed to be the best pistol shot in the parish. Wright was a noted duelist, having engaged in at least five duels and killed his man in two of them. The differences between Bowie and Wright were many. When Wright had made a successful race for sheriff of Rapides Parish, he had been opposed by Sam Wells. Bowie had supported his friend Wells, whose cousin he had been engaged to. In addition, Wright belonged to a group of men competing with the Bowies in their land speculation ventures. To make matters worse, Wright was director of a bank from which Bowie had borrowed money. When he tried to make another loan in order to stave off a piece of valuable property from foreclosure, Wright was instrumental in having the loan rejected.[1]

One day the two enemies accidentally met on the street in Alexandria. Without warning, Wright pulled out his pistol and fired at Bowie. One story has it that the ball struck Bowie but was deflected by a silver dollar in his breast pocket, thus saving his life. Furious, Bowie drew his own pistol and tried to fire it, but the gun misfired. Another story has it that James was unarmed.

Regardless, Bowie waded into Wright and would have killed the major with his bare hands if friends had not intervened.

The attack so enraged Bowie that he had a leather scabbard made for his hunting knife and swore that he would wear the knife for the rest of his life.[2] From then on, everyone in Alexandria considered the two enemies as walking time bombs and wondered when the expected explosion would take place. That event was to occur a year later in the famous Battle of the Sandbar.

Formal, pre-arranged duels with strict rules and regulations had long been legal in the United States. These were usually fought with pistols or swords and were fought for a variety of reasons: in defense of one's honor; to avenge fancied slights or wrongs; to settle enmities or disputes concerning political differences; to fight for the affections of a lady; or for any reason under the sun.

Under the *code duello* one could not challenge an intended opponent; all negotiations had to be handled through a second, and the challenged had the choice of weapons. As late as 1836 the *code duello* was still being printed.[3]

Dueling was widespread during the early 1800s, and many men of distinction were not hesitant to challenge or accept a challenge to settle their grievances. The venerable Henry Clay, secretary of state, had engaged in a duel with John Randolph, and the fiery, hot-tempered Andrew Jackson, before becoming president of the United States, once engaged in a duel and killed a man who was foolish enough to make a slighting remark about Mrs. Jackson. Sam Houston, while a congressman from Tennessee and before serving as commander-in-chief of the Texas forces in the Texas War for Independence against Mexico, once fought a duel with pistols over a political controversy.[4]

Perhaps the most famous duel on record in the United States was one fought between Aaron Burr, then serving as vice-president under Thomas Jefferson, and Alexander Hamilton, who had been George Washington's brilliant secretary of the treasury. The duel, which was fought with pistols, was the culmination of months of political differences of opinion between the two men. Hamilton, who was vigorously opposed to dueling, accepted a challenge by Burr and on July 11, 1804, the two men met at Weehawken, New Jersey, on the same spot where Hamilton's son had been killed in a duel three years previously. In the encounter with Burr, Hamilton was mortally wounded and died the next day.[5]

Although legal, dueling was by no means universally accepted. Many editorials in the nation's newspapers continually raged against the practice during the early 1800s. Churches and many secular organizations, including the Masonic lodge, were opposed to the practice. Houston, a Mason, while governor of Tennessee was suspended from his lodge in Nashville for his duel. He appealed to the Grand Lodge of Tennessee but that body upheld his suspension.[6]

With the public clamor against the practice of dueling, many states, including Texas, had passed laws against it prior to 1840. There was also considerable support in Congress for similar federal legislation.

Today one might wonder why men would fight duels over what were seemingly inconsequential matters. Times were different then. The nation was still young, and many people still lived on the frontier or on the edge of it, far from the law. Men were accustomed to settling their differences in person — not to running to court to sue over every trivial matter. Perhaps another compelling reason why men who loathed the very thought of dueling would accept a challenge was because to refuse to do so would brand a man as a coward and set him up to be treated with contempt by those who knew him.

For years the Vidalia sandbar, named for Joseph Vidal, a French settler who owned Concordia, had been a favorite place for men to settle their differences by dueling. It was on this sandbar that Gen. Winfield Scott of the United States Army had met one Dr. Upshaw after Scott had criticized Capt. James Wilkinson. Governor George Poindexter of Mississippi, in a duel with pistols, had claimed the life of Abijah Hunt, and Maj. Ferdinand Claiborne had engaged in a duel with Capt. Benjamin Farar. Many others with various scores to settle had drawn their pistols on this lonely stretch.

It was at high noon September 19, 1827, when the quietness of this lonely sandbar on Shillings Bayou, on the Mississippi River a few miles west of Natchez, was to be shattered by the sounds of guns firing as men met in mortal combat.

The two men whose enmity resulted in the duel on this forsaken place, as well as their seconds, surgeons and witnesses, were all well respected and men of good standing and influence in their communities. On one side, as duelist, was Samuel Levi Wells III; his second was Maj. George C. McWhorter, and Dr. Richard Cuny was his surgeon. Others of his party consisted of his brother, Thomas Jefferson Wells, James Bowie, and Gen. Samuel Cuny, who was brother to Dr. Cuny. Bowie, the Cunys, and the Wells were cousins, and James had been engaged to Cecelia Wells, sister of the Wells brothers. She had died two weeks prior to the wedding.

Samuel Wells' opponent was Dr. Thomas Harris Maddox, originally from Charles County, Maryland. Dr. James A. Denny was serving as surgeon for Dr. Maddox, and Col. Robert Alexander Crain, originally of Fauquier County, Virginia, served as Maddox's "friend," or second. The rest of the Maddox party consisted of Bowie's old enemy Maj. Norris Wright, who hailed from Baltimore, Maryland; the brothers Alfred and Edward Cary Blanchard of Norfolk, Virginia, who were related by marriage to Colonel Crain; John B. Nevitt, Dr. William R. Provan, Thomas Hunt, Col. William Barnard, who carried a shotgun, and Dr. William R. Cox. Last of the group was Colonel Crain's young servant, who was to carry two pistols belonging to his master.

For many reasons the Bowie, Wells, Cuny group and the Maddox, Crain, Blanchard, and Wright faction had long held much hatred toward each other. Their bitterness was well known to the people of Alexandria and its environs. Several of the individuals who made the trip to the sandbar had their own individual ax to grind against at least one member of the opposing group.

Part of the feud resulted from Samuel Cuny, then being lieutenant of horse, having been appointed brigadier general in the militia over Colonel Crain, who resented the fact that he had not received the appointment. The supporters of each man promptly took sides in the matter, and the feud became exceedingly bitter.

In addition to the promotion incident, General Cuny and Colonel Crain had long been bitter foes. The colonel was exceedingly slow in paying his bills and frequently would issue a challenge to his creditor upon receiving a bill. The father of General Cuny, Richmond E. Cuny, had made the mistake of endorsing a note for the colonel. When Crain would not pay the note the Cunys had to sell some of their slaves to raise funds to honor the endorsement. General Cuny was so enraged by Crain's action that in a shooting incident near the Cuny plantation he wounded the colonel in the left arm, while Crain's shot went astray. From that moment on there was hatred between the two families.[7]

A Dr. John C. Rippey once refused to accept Crain's note in payment of some rent due on a plantation. Angered, Colonel Crain then killed the doctor in a duel. This killing caused a schism between the Crain and Wells families, inasmuch as nieces of Mrs. Rippey were married to Gen. Montford Wells and his brother, Thomas Jefferson Wells.

There were others in the opposing groups who had their differences. While intoxicated at a ballroom dance, Alfred Blanchard had stabbed Thomas Jefferson Wells; the wound, how-ever, proved not to be serious. And then, of course, there were the old foes, James Bowie and Norris Wright. Once more they would come to grips.

The particular catalyst that brought on the celebrated affair at the sandbar was the result of a scandal concerning Mary Wells, sister to the Wells brothers. According to a story making the rounds of Alexandria, Louisiana, a patient of Dr. Maddox re-peated a piece of sordid gossip concerning Mary Wells and the doctor lost no time in repeating the tale. The story infuriated the three Wells brothers — General Montfort (eldest of the trio), Samuel, and Thomas Jefferson. The general was the first to react and proceeded to ask Maddox for the name of his informant. Maddox refused to give the name, stating only that his informant was a woman. The two men then engaged in a quarrel, with mu-tual insults and deadly threats being exchanged. Two weeks later, the two met on the streets of Alexandria. General Wells, armed with a shotgun, pulled both triggers. Since he had cataracts his vision was none too good, and his shotgun blast succeeded in killing only the usual "innocent" bystander. Maddox escaped un-scathed and ran to his nearby office.

Not too long thereafter a messenger carried the doctor's note of challenge to General Wells. The general declined on the grounds that "he only met his equals on the field of honor." Shortly thereafter, Maddox received an acceptance to his chal-lenge, but from Samuel Levi Wells. The latter pointed out that his brother was an old man with very poor eyesight and pleurisy and that he, Samuel, would be more than happy to render satisfaction to Maddox. Under the code in force at that time, substitutions were acceptable if allowed by the challenger. The doctor agreed to the substitution, and on September 17 and 18, 1827, conferences between representatives of both participants met. At the conferences rules were arranged and seconds and witnesses were selected. According to the terms agreed upon, each participant was allowed one shot. If no one was injured, a brief pause would be held; then another shot would be allowed, and regardless of the outcome the duel would end.

As the sandbar was some seventy miles northeast of Alexandria, it might seem odd that two men intent on fighting a duel would travel so far from their place of residence. But perhaps the reason this forlorn patch of ground was chosen is that both factions were anticipating a general battle to give them a chance to settle long-festering sores. The friction between the two groups was high due to the many political, business, and personal differences among both sides. As it turned out, the arranged duel between challenger and challenged was just a prelude to what was to follow.

At noon on September 19, 1827, as the sun was shining over nearby Natchez across the river, Samuel Wells and Dr. Thomas Maddox faced each other at the agreed upon ten paces. Major McWhorter and Colonel Crain, the two seconds, took their appointed places with pistols in hand. Doctors Cuny and Denny stood nearby with their medical bags to render aid if necessary. Those six were the only ones on the field of battle. Members of the opposing factions who were witnessing the event stood many yards away in separate copes of willows to await the outcome of the duel. Colonel Barnard of the Maddox faction, and who had a double-barreled shotgun, had piloted his group through an intricate swamp to reach their position in the woods.

When Samuel Wells and Dr. Maddox fired their first shots, they missed. The two opponents fired again, and once more their bullets went astray. Wells and Maddox then advanced toward each other and, honor being satisfied, shook hands. Samuel Wells then invited Dr. Maddox and his party to go to the woods, where the rest of his party was, and drink a glass of wine. Colonel Crain objected, stating there were certain parties in the other group he could not meet with; thereupon Dr. Maddox invited the group to go where his friends were and have the drink of wine. Wells agreed, and the six men then started walking toward the Maddox faction.

As the small group walked toward the distant woods, they met the remaining two factions, with James Bowie, General Cuny, and Thomas Jefferson Wells leading. As the two parties approached each other, General Cuny called out to Colonel Crain: "This is a good time to settle our own problems, here and now."[8] While speaking, he started to draw his pistol. According to a statement made by Colonel Crain, published in the *Natchez Ariel-Extra* on October 19, 1827, he immediately fired at James Bowie and wounded him in the hip. Cuny now had his pistol out, and he and the colonel fired simultaneously. Cuny's bullet grazed Crain in his left arm, but Crain's bullet struck General Cuny's left breast and left him dying on the sand.

Bowie had been knocked off his feet by Crain's bullet. In spite of the wound in his hip he managed to arise and, drawing a large knife (described as a butcher knife) charged toward his attacker. Crain waited until he came within reach and, clubbing his empty pistol, struck Bowie on the head with such a terrible blow that Bowie sank to his knees and Crain's pistol broke. Dr. Maddox then jumped on Bowie and held him down for some moments before James, collecting his strength, managed to throw Maddox off him. In the meantime, Crain had taken to his heels.[9]

While this fracas was going on, Maj. Norris Wright had appeared on the scene and quickly took a shot at Bowie, who returned his fire. One account states Bowie hit Norris, who exclaimed "the damned rascal has killed me." Regardless, the major still had strength enough left to draw his sword-cane. He approached the prostrate Bowie and plunged the stilleto-like blade into James' chest, pinning him to the ground. He then attempted to withdraw the blade by placing one foot upon Bowie and pulling on his sword. Alfred Blanchard also started stabbing Bowie with his sword-cane. James then seized Wright and jerked him downward. After plunging his knife into his enemy's body he pulled upward and disemboweled Wright, who promptly died. Bowie would later remark: "I twisted the knife until I heard his heart-strings sing." He then wearily rose to his feet and tried to withdraw the slender sword from his chest.

Both of the Blanchard brothers now bore down on the thrice-injured Bowie and tried to finish him off by shooting at him, and Carey Blanchard shot him in the hip. James, with four separate wounds by four different foes, still refused to give up. He rushed at Alfred Blanchard and once more called upon his knife. This time, he stripped the flesh from Blanchard's forearm. Blanchard turned and ran toward his brother Carey, who fired at Bowie again but missed. The two brothers tried to flee the scene, but as they were running away George McWhorter shot and wounded Carey Blanchard. Dr. Maddox and most of his friends now left the scene of the battle but stayed on the island. The Battle of the Sandbar was over, and the entire affair had lasted about ten minutes.

Bowie was in precarious shape. He had lost much blood due to his various wounds, and Wright's sword blade still protruded from his chest. As he fell to the ground once more his friends surrounded him. Dr. Cuny had been attending to the wound of his brother until the general died. The doctor then brought out his large forceps and withdrew the sword from Bowie. With medicines and bandages taken from his kit, he staunched James' flow of blood. With his probe and scalpel he then removed the bullets that Bowie had absorbed in his arm and hip.

Colonel Crain, who had returned to the scene, took some water to Bowie, his adversary. James thanked him but added he did not think Crain had acted properly in firing upon him when he was exchanging shots with Maddox. In later years the two men became reconciled, and had great respect for each other.[10]

The Wells party improvised a willow stretcher, placed Bowie on it, and then boarded a boat to Concordia on the Louisiana side. As the boat crossed the river, their erstwhile opponents hid among the willows.

There was no victor in the Battle of the Sandbar. Out of the total party of sixteen, the two principal antagonists both missed their allotted two shots. Each faction had one man killed in the general melee that followed; and, in addition to Bowie, Crain and both Blanchard brothers were wounded. Even Dr. Denny, the surgeon for Dr. Maddox, suffered a couple of wounds from passing bullets, although the injuries were of a minor nature.

Bowie and his friends eventually returned to Natchez, and he stayed in that city for months recuperating from his wounds.

Most likely, the only thing that saved him from dying was his sturdy, rugged constitution and his tremendous will to live.

After the guns ceased firing and the survivors of the battle made their way back to town, it wasn't long before newspapers carried headlines reporting the events of that fateful day. The name of James Bowie and his part in the affair was mentioned prominently.

On September 24, 1827, Samuel Wells wrote the *New Orleans Argus,* giving his version of the events that took place only five days previously. In his letter Wells made the assertion that Colonel Crain, among his Natchez friends, had stated that he would kill General Cuny on sight if Cuny made his appearance on the ground; in any event, he planned to kill him at the first opportunity. On October 3 Colonel Crain wrote a letter to his friend Gen. Joseph Marshall Walker, a Bayou Rapides planter who later became the first governor of Louisiana, giving his version of the events that transpired. At the same time he denied making the remark attributed to him that he planned to kill General Cuny.

During the month of October, the *Ariel-Extra* of Natchez carried a statement of the affair from Colonel Crain, who described the knife Bowie used as "a big knife."[11] The *Ariel* also carried versions of the affair from various members of the Maddox group, and they also described Bowie's weapon as "a big knife." Dr. Thomas Hunt, John B. Nevitt, Col. William Barnard, and Doctors James Denny, William Cox, and William Provan were all heard from. Both Denny and Nevitt described Bowie's knife as "a large knife." The New Orleans *Argus* of October 2, 1827, described the weapon as "a large butcher knife." The October 27, 1827, edition of the *National Gazette and Literary Register,* a Philadelphia newspaper, carried Sam Wells' version of the affair. The November 17 *Niles Register* of Washington, D.C. quickly followed with a version of the duel by someone who signed himself as "An Eye Witness." As late as March 1860, in the *Concordia* (Louisiana) *Intelligencer* there appeared a very interesting account of that fateful day in 1827 from someone who signed himself as "W. P. M." He mentioned "the peculiar shaped and formidable knife used by Col. Bowie." Throughout the years there have been many versions of the duels by people claiming to have been eyewitnesses of the duel, but most of them are obviously false.

Although there were some minor discrepancies by those
actually on the sandbar and who either participated in the melee
or witnessed it, on all major points everyone agreed. And one
thing the Maddox-Crain-Blanchard faction agreed on was that
everyone attacked James Bowie first and concentrated on trying
to kill him because they considered him the most dangerous man
among their opposition.

Of all participants in the duel and its bloody aftermath the
last one to be heard from was Dr. Thomas H. Maddox, who by
unwisely repeating a bit of gossip was responsible for the whole
affair taking place. The doctor finally died in 1888 at the age of
ninety-five. Not making a public statement at the time of the duel,
in 1880 he gave to a New Orleans newspaper his version of those
events that happened fifty-three years previously. His version
largely agreed with the other participants on the major points of
the afternoon. He, like other members of his faction, agreed that
everyone considered Bowie to be their most dangerous opponent, and the doctor referred to Bowie as the "Major General of
the party."

There may be some dispute as to whether this is the first
time James Bowie ever used the famous Bowie knife, but there is
no doubt that the deadly way he wielded the knife while fighting
for his life gave him the start of his reputation as a deadly fighting
man and made his name a household word in the Southwest. It
was the beginning of a reputation he was never entirely to live
down, and from then on the story of his life would be based partly
on fact and partly on myth.

CHAPTER 6

Who Invented
the Bowie Knife?

J ust who invented the Bowie knife, and when? Was it a common hunting knife, or a butcher knife of that time, as some authors suggest? What were its antecedents? What did it look like? Did it have a guard on the handle? Who were those parties that manufactured the knife, or its many versions, and where are some of the famous Bowie knives today? These are questions many authors and historians have been debating for years.

There is another question of interest to many people. Was the original Bowie knife used by James Bowie in the famous Battle of the Sandbar, or did it come into being later on?

Knives, of course, were nothing new in the history of hunting or warfare. The ancient Moors had long used them in their campaigns, and for years the Spanish dirk had been a familiar weapon in Spain. Native Americans had used stone knives in their hunting and scalping until metal knives were introduced to them along the Eastern seaboard more than three centuries ago by the English. No doubt the Spaniards similarly introduced metal knives to the Indians of the Southwest as they marched through that region of America.

Many men have been credited with inventing the first Bowie knife, among them Jesse Cliffe, a blacksmith in the employ of Rezin P. Bowie. (Although his name was actually "Clifft," in most accounts it is spelled "Cliffe.") Capt. Rees Fitzpatrick, a gunsmith of Natchez, has been credited with its invention, as has been one "Pedro." A blacksmith named Lovel H. Snowden has his adherents, as does a smith known as "Manuel." An "unknown" Philadelphia cutler is given credit, as is a Mr. Sowell.

Probably the three names most frequently mentioned as being the inventor of the famous blade are those of James Bowie himself, his brother Rezin, and James Black, a well-known and skilled blacksmith who lived in Washington, Hempstead County, Arkansas.

The *Galveston Daily News* of March 31, 1890, gave a version of James Bowie having the famous knife made. This version was given by Miss Annie M. Bowie, a granddaughter of the John Bowie who was the brother of Rezin, Sr. She based her account upon "material obtained from annals of my branch of the family." According to Miss Bowie, "James had the knife made by Lovel H. Snowden, with the intention of using it to defend the rights of a widow who was about to be defrauded of a Spanish grant by certain planters." She implied that they were the same men against whom he employed the knife in the sandbar affair.[1]

Among the various stories connecting James Bowie with originating the knife that bears his name, two are presented by J. Frank Dobie, noted Texas historian. In one version, Dobie related that in preparation for the sandbar duel, James Bowie himself took a fourteen-inch file to a cutler in New Orleans known as Pedro. Pedro had learned his trade in Toledo, "where the finest swords in all Spain were forged, and all his skill went into the making of a blade which was to be, in Bowie's words, 'fit to fight for a man's life with.'"[2]

The second version once more connects Snowden with making the knife for James but sometime *after* the sandbar fight. Dobie continued: "Yet another story avers that while recovering from wounds sustained in the famous fight, James Bowie whittled from soft wood a pattern of the knife that was to make his own name historic, and had a blacksmith named Lovel Snowden fashion the weapon."[3]

John J. Bowie was another one who placed credence in the story that Snowden first made the knife for Jim.

> He had a hunting knife made [according to John] which suited his fancy, by a common blacksmith named Snowden. In after years this knife became famous, owing to some very tragical occurrences which originated as follows: About the year 1826 James became involved in the political and party squabbles of the day, and his fiery, impulsive nature caused him to enlist all his energies in the strife. At this time he resided in Alexandria,

on Red River, and in some of the momentary excitement of the day, an altercation took place between him and the sheriff of Rapides Parish, a Mr. Norris Wright, during which Wright shot Bowie in his left breast, while he was unarmed; but had Wright not been rescued by his friends James would have killed him with his fists. This attack so enraged him that he had a neat leather scabbard made for his hunting knife, and affirmed that he would wear it as long as he lived, which he did. About twelve months after this difficulty, or in September, 1827, the great duel took place at Natchez.[4]

The *Encyclopedia Americana* of 1928 had its say on the matter: "Colonel James Bowie is said to have had his sword broken down to within about twenty inches of the hilt in a fight with some Mexicans, but he found that he did such good execution with his broken blade that he equipped all his followers with a similar weapon -- the Bowie knife."[5]

Most authorities on the Bowie knife tend to believe it was invented by James' brother Rezin. Lucy Leigh Bowie of Washington, D.C., a relative of Col. James Bowie, prepared an article which was read at the meeting of the Bucks County Historical Society held in Doylestown, Pennsylvania, on June 17, 1916. The article gave some brief facts about the life of Bowie and was published in the *Daily Intelligencer* of Doylestown three days later. In the article, Lucy Bowie made some comments about the famous Bowie knife and gave Rezin credit for both its design and its invention.

In 1827, the Bowie knife was not a new invention. It had been made for Rezin P. Bowie before he left his father's home in Opelousas. He had been attacked once when he attempted to plunge his hunting knife into the head of a bullock, but the oncoming rush of the enraged animal drove the knife back into his hand, which was impaled against the horn, severely wounding his hand and almost severing the thumb. This could not have occurred had the knife possessed a guard; so Rezin Bowie had a new one made from an old file to his own fancies by Jesse Cliffe, a white blacksmith on his plantation. This knife had a straight blade nine and-a-quarter inches long and one and-a-half inches wide, with a single edge to the guard. Rezin used this in hunting and found the steel wonderfully true, and the shape made it much more reliable for personal defense than either the sword cane, or the Spanish dagger, both of which were in Universal use at that period, and both were afterwards superceded by the Bowie knife.

Later in her article she mentions that James and Rezin made a trip north, and while in Philadelphia Rezin sought out a cutler and gave him a model of the knife. The cutler improved it by shortening the blade to eight inches, putting a curve in one side of the point, and sharpening both edges. He then put the blade on the market.

According to the *Houston Post* of February 16, 1936, it was James who cut his hand badly while hunting wild cattle in the Attacapa country. While using an ordinary hunting knife, his hand slipped from the handle down upon the blade. "Hunting knives," he complained, "ought to have a guard between the handle and the blade. If there had been one on this knife, I wouldn't have cut myself." This gave Rezin an idea. He sought out Jesse Cliffe, a white blacksmith he employed on his planta-tion, and had him fashion a knife from a large, broad file, with a guard between blade and handle. This, according to the article, was the knife Jim used to kill Maj. Norris Wright in the celebrated fight.

Andrew J. Sowell, a former captain in the Texas Rangers, was one claiming it was James who conceived the idea of putting a guard on the knife when he severely cut his hand. Sowell, rely-ing on family tradition, claimed that the knife came into being in Gonzales, Texas, since James frequently came through that town while in Texas. He was usually accompanied by a party of men, and he and his friends were often involved in fights with Indians. Sowell wrote:

> In one of these thrusts Bowie made a thrust at an Indian when they were at close quarters, and his hand slipped over the blade of his butcher knife, cutting him severely. This mishap suggested the idea of a guard between the blade and handle, and he determined to have one made that way. Accordingly, selecting a piece of wood, he made a pattern of the kind of knife he wanted, and the next time he went to Gonzales, he went to Mr. Sowell's shop, and showing him the pattern, asked if he could make one like it. The old man said he thought he could, and selecting a good piece of steel, proceeded to shape one like the pattern, and after it was finished, presented it to Bowie for

inspection. He was greatly pleased with it, and paid a handsome price for the work. The old man then asked Bowie if he might name the knife. "Oh, yes, Mr. Sowell, certainly," said Bowie, "give it a name." "Well, then," said the old man, "I will name it in honor of you. We will call it the Bowie knife."[6]

Maj. Horace Shelton is one who agreed with Lucy Leigh Bowie that it was Rezin whose hand slipped and injured his fingers badly. "Rezin, not James, designed the Bowie knife," he stated, and further explained:

> After a long, hard chase, and after lassoing and throwing a wild bull, Rezin leaped from his horse for the kill. He was using a butcher knife and as he stabbed the bull in the neck the blade's point struck bone. His hand slipped from the handle to the cutting edge, almost severing two of his fingers. He remarked to James: "We need cross-bars on our knives. Let's make a better knife." Rezin made a sketch of his idea and the first knife was made by a blacksmith on the Louisiana plantation. But it was young James, not Rezin, who first baptized the knife in blood and gave it a name among knives as significant as that which Samuel Colt later gave to the six-shooting pistol.[7]

In addition to Lucy Leigh Bowie, a great number of Bowie family members, all of them having access to family papers and documents not generally available to the public, consider Rezin P. Bowie as inventor of the knife bearing the Bowie name. Among them are Dr. J. Moore Soniat du Fosset of New Orleans, who was a great-grandson of Rezin and Margaret Neville Bowie. According to notes kept by du Fosset, the Bowie brothers were very fond of riding wild cattle down, a popular sport among planters of Louisiana at the time. One method of subduing the wild animals was to shoot them from horseback; a second method was to lasso and then stab them. This was the method preferred by the Bowies.

> One day while Rezin was thrusting his knife into a ferocious bull, the animal lunged in such a way as to draw the blade through his hand, making a very severe wound. It was after he had his hand dressed that Rezin called for his plantation blacksmith, Jesse Cliffe. With a pencil, he traced on paper a blade some ten inches long and two inches broad at its widest part, the handle to be strong and well protected from the blade by guards. He then gave Cliffe a large file of the best quality

steel and instructed him to make a knife out of it. The knife was very serviceable in hunting, and Rezin prized it so highly he kept it locked in his desk when he was not wearing it.

Dr. du Fosset's account goes on to tell that one day James Bowie told Rezin how he had been attacked by Major Wright, and how his own pistol had failed to fire when he attempted to defend himself. Rezin then unlocked his desk, took out his prized personal possession, and handed it to his brother, saying: "Here, James take 'Old Bowie.' She never misses fire."[8]

Apparently James eventually returned "Old Bowie" to his brother, as for many years the knife remained in Rezin's family as an heirloom. It was later lost when one of Rezin's grandsons took it with him on a fishing trip and the boat capsized on Bayou Pierre. Dr. du Fosset later wrote that ". . . even now it lies at the bottom of a stream. The silver tip of the scabbard is still in the possession of the descendants who reside in New Orleans."

John S. Moore, a merchant of New Orleans, was a grandson of Rezin, and was in possession of his grandfather's papers and manuscripts. Consequently, he had a broad and presumably accurate knowledge of the Louisiana Bowies. In a letter of April 25, 1890, to W. W. Fontaine, he wrote that it was his grandfather who had the knife made for the use of James. He described the weapon as being eight and a quarter inches long and one and a quarter inches wide, with a curved point, and sharp on only one edge. This knife, stated Moore, was the one James used in the sandbar duel.[9]

Rezin P. Bowie certainly did not hesitate to take credit for the invention of the famous knife.

On June 9 and June 11, 1838, the *Baltimore Commercial Transcript* published articles by a gentleman signing himself as "P. Q." The articles mentioned duels in which both James and Rezin purportedly participated, and described the Bowie knife as having a blade measuring twelve inches in length and being two inches broad at the heel and of proportionate thickness. The point was curved and hollowed at the back, cutting both ways, like a two-edged sword. "P. Q." went on to describe the edge as keen and smooth and so perfect that a barber might use it in his trade.

Rezin considered the articles so slanderous and rife with erroneous information that in a letter written from Iberville, Louisiana, and dated August 24, 1838, he wrote to the editor of *The*

Planters' Advocate in defense of himself and James, and repudiated the remarks made by "P. Q." In his lengthy reply, Rezin unequivocally claimed he had invented the Bowie knife, and gave his version:

> ... The first Bowie knife was made by myself in the parish of Avoyelles, in this state, as a hunting knife, for which purpose, exclusively, it was used for many years. The length of the knife was nine and one-quarter inches, its width one and a half inches, single edge, and blade not curved; so the "Correspondent" is as incorrect in his description as in his account of the original of the "Bowie-Knife." The Baltimore correspondent must have been greatly misinformed respecting the manner in which Col. James Bowie first became possessed of this knife, or he must possess a very fertile imagination. The whole of his statement on this point is false.
>
> The following are the facts:
>
> Colonel James Bowie had been shot by an individual with whom he was at variance; and as I presumed that a second attempt would be made by the same person to take his life, I gave him the knife to be used as occasion might require, as a defensive weapon. Some time afterwards (and the only time the knife was ever used for any purpose other than that for which it was intended, or originally destined) it was resorted to by Colonel James Bowie in a chance medley, or rough fight, between himself and certain other individuals with whom he was then inimical, and the knife was then used only as a defensive weapon — and not till he had been shot down; it was then the means of saving his life. The improvement in its fabrication, and the state of perfection which it has since acquired from experienced cutlers, was not brought about through my agency. I would here assert also, that neither Col. James Bowie nor myself at any period in our lives, ever had a duel with any person soever.

It is regrettable that Rezin did not give the date he had his hunting knife made, or state whether or not it had a cross-guard on the handle. As he admits the knife was only a hunting knife and does not mention any guard between the blade and the handle, but does mention the blade was later on improved, it seems likely the guard was added to the knife later on.

Rezin's description of his invention certainly does not resemble the popular conception of what a "classic" Bowie knife looks like, which conceives of the weapon having a familiar concave clip point, sharp false edge cut from both sides, and a cross-guard to protect the hand. The knife Rezin described very closely resembles the "Spanish dagger," which had long been used in the South and Southwest. The main difference between the two was that the knife Rezin designed had a wider blade than the Spanish dagger, and the heel of the blade, where it joined the hilt, was wider than the hilt.

Rezin was being very gracious when he referred to the affair on the sandbar as a "chance medley." Certainly the duel between Wells and Dr. Maddox was a planned affair, and very likely there was a general understanding between the participants in the imbroglio that followed that they would settle their differences with their enemies when the main event was over.

It is highly unlikely that so many men would meet so far away from their home surroundings in a "chance medley," and perhaps one reason they chose such a lonely spot was the embarrassment that would occur to Norris Wright, who was sheriff of his parish, if he was in a duel that occurred in his own bailiwick.

Nor was Rezin being entirely truthful when he claimed that neither his brother nor himself, at any period in their lives, ever had a duel with "any person soever." Perhaps he didn't, but James certainly did, and in more than one instance.

In a letter dated September 14, 1885, to Col. David F. Boyd, Mrs. Eugene Sonniat, granddaughter of Rezin, confirmed his claim of having been first to make the knife. "This instrument," she wrote, "was made of an old file in the plantation blacksmith shop of my grandfather's Bayou Boeuf plantation, the maker was a hired white man named Jesse Clift [*sic*] he afterwards went to Texas. My mother, Mrs. Jos. H. Moore, then a little girl, went to the shop with her father, heard his directions, and saw Clift make the knife."[10]

Regardless of who actually invented the first Bowie knife, it and its later models proved to be a fierce weapon in the hands of a fighting man, and doubly so in the hands of a skilled fighting machine such as James Bowie.

CHAPTER 7

The Saga of James Black

R egardless of who made the first Bowie knife, it bore little resemblance to the modern perception of what a classic Bowie knife looks like. And it has certainly undergone much evolution since the first one made under Rezin's supervision came from a blacksmith's forge, with a straight blade and no long, concave, curved point.

According to Raymond W. Thorp in his book *Bowie Knife,* the knife used by Bowie in the fracas on the sandbar was a common butcher knife as the dreaded Bowie knife had not yet been invented.[1] According to Thorp, the knife was actually invented some three years after the sandbar incident by one James Black, who developed and forged a knife with a curved forward blade and a short, dagger-like backhand blade, all in steel of the most wonderful tempering.[2] Thorp is not alone in his belief that Black was the inventor of the famed weapon.

The saga of James Black is a fascinating one indeed, and has all the elements of drama: love and hate, success and failure, tragedy and pathos.

Daniel Webster Jones, the son of Dr. Isaac N. Jones, was a lawyer, served as an officer in the Confederate army, and later served two terms as governor of Arkansas from 1897 to 1901. When young Daniel was a child, James Black came to live with the family of Dr. Jones and stayed with them until he died in 1872. During the thirty years he was a guest of the Jones family, Black and Daniel had many conversations. In 1903, at the age of sixty-three, Jones wrote his reminiscences and had a portion devoted to his friend Black. The manuscript lay long unpublished, but finally a sketch pertaining to Black saw the light of day in the *Arkansas Gazette* of November 20, 1919. The sketch related Black's early life and particularly to his claim as being the inventor of the first Bowie knife as we know it.

As former Governor Jones told the story, Black was born May 1, 1800, in a village in New Jersey. His mother died when he was four, and four years later his father remarried. As young Black and his stepmother did not get along, the youth ran away to Philadelphia and was quickly taken into custody by the authorities. As he refused to tell anyone where he came from, they decided to place him with a man named Henderson, who was a manufacturer of silverplated ware.

The young man became an apt pupil and accomplished in the silverplating business. At age eighteen, with his apprenticeship over, he decided to move westward and ended up in New Orleans, where he secured a job as deck hand on a steamer headed for the Red River. While on the steamer he became friends with one Elijah Stuart. When they debarked the vessel at Fulton, on the Red River, the two of them went inland about fourteen miles and settled in Washington, Hempstead County, Arkansas, in the early spring of 1824. The place they chose for their new home was on the old Chihuahua Trail to Texas.

While Stuart established a tavern, Black quickly found employment with a blacksmith named William Shaw. In those days no community could get along without the village blacksmith; he was an important man in both business and social circles. Shaw and his two eldest sons operated a successful business and were busy shoeing horses, re-tiring wagon wheels, repairing plows, and doing all the incidental work a smith did in those days. Black, for his part, was to devote his entire time to the making and mending of guns and knives, as that was a substantial portion of the business of most frontier blacksmiths.

Black quickly proved to be a very skilled gunsmith and knifemaker, as well as silverplater. The tall, handsome young Black proved to be popular within the Washington community and got along very well with Mr. Shaw and his sons, particularly with the older son. With Shaw's business increasing due to Black's skill and popularity, the older man soon took Black in as an equal

partner. Perhaps he did so to eliminate the possibility of the popular, highly skilled Black from opening up his own shop and going
into competition with him. As partners the two men got along
very well and the business flourished. Then love entered the
picture.

Anne, the oldest of the Shaw daughters, was some years
younger than James Black. Intelligent and quite pretty, she was
one of the belles of Washington and had plenty of beaux. However, she fell in love with Black and the two soon wanted to get
married. From then on, Black told Jones, things started sliding
downhill.

For some reason, perhaps because he thought Anne could
do better, Shaw vigorously opposed the marriage and forbade his
daughter to marry his young partner. Black reasoned that in time
Shaw would relent, and he secured a promise from Anne that she
would marry him in the future. He sold his share of the business
to Shaw and in the transaction proved that skillful as he was as a
blacksmith, silverplater, gun repairer and maker of knives, he was
a novice when it came to business. Instead of insisting upon being
paid in cash for his share of the business, he took a 400-day note.

Without funds, Black then moved further west into the wilderness and built a cabin at the Rolling Fork of the Cossatot River.
Other adventurers joined him within a few months. As the small
settlement grew, Black decided to erect a dam in the river and
build a grist mill. As he had virtually no money, he went into debt
with his friends and talked them into helping him on the project.

The dam and mill were almost completed when fate struck
Black another blow. One day the sheriff arrived and read a proclamation from President Andrew Jackson that they were on
Indian property and would have to leave at once. Without funds
to pay his workers and terribly in debt, Black decided the only
thing he could do was to swallow his pride, return to Washington, and go back to work for Shaw as an employee. Shaw accepted
him back, but when Black attempted to collect some of the money
due him for the sale of his partnership, he discovered that legally
he was entitled to nothing. The papers he had signed dissolving
the partnership made no mention at all of any financial consideration.

With nothing to lose, Black and Anne Shaw were married in
Washington on June 29, 1828,[3] and subsequently became par-

ents of five children: sons William Jefferson, Grandison, John Colburt, and Sydonham, and daughter Sarah Jane.[4]

After the wedding, Black secured some financial backing and set up a blacksmith and metal-working business in opposition to his new father-in-law. This further incurred Shaw's hatred, according to the story, but Black's marriage was a happy and successful one and from the start he prospered with his own shop.

In those days the West was far from tamed, and most men, law-abiding or not, carried a knife. It was the custom for each customer to furnish a pattern, which was usually made of wood or cardboard, for the sort of knife he desired. With his own business, it didn't take Black long before he quickly secured a reputation as a maker of knives of a superior quality with razor-sharp blades.

According to observers, Black did not consider one of his blades to be worthy of his skill until it passed the "hickory test." After a blade was finished, Black would whittle on a seasoned hickory block for thirty minutes. Then, if it would not smoothly shave the hair from his arm, the knife would be discarded.[5]

Black not only gave his blades superior steel and sharpness, but with his skill as a silverplater plated his weapons with precious metals and odd and beautiful designs. He charged prices as high as $52, depending on the amount of gold and silver used and the particular design desired. His lowest priced knife, for which a charge of $5 was made, had neither plating nor engraving, yet it ranked in quality with those selling for a much higher price.[6]

It wasn't long before Black had more business than he could handle, so he took one of his brothers-in-law into the business with him. Yet he never allowed young Shaw to learn his special technique of tempering and hardening the steel. It was claimed that he knew the famous Damascus secret of resiliency, temper, and cutting edge for their swords, and he did not want to share this knowledge with anyone. From what he told the future Governor Jones, he had no idea how he acquired the Damascus secret. It just came to him mysteriously, as his training was in plating iron and steel and not making them.

Black protected his secret very well. When curious onlookers would come into his smithy to observe him at work and perhaps obtain some knowledge of how he managed to impart so much sharpness into his blades, he would never let anyone get very close to him.

Now James Bowie enters the picture. It was early in December of 1830, and Bowie was riding to visit Rezin at the latter's plantation at Walnut Hills, Arkansas. The skill of James Black as a master knife craftsman had penetrated Texas, and James stopped in Washington to order one of the famed knives. He presented Black with a model he had whittled and asked him to follow that design. Stating he would return in several weeks, he then rode on to his brother's plantation.

When Bowie returned to the blacksmith's shop to pick up his new purchase, he was shown two knives by Black. One was made according to the Bowie specifications; the other one was one Black had designed himself. Bowie could look the two over and take his pick of the one he decided was the best. The price would be the same regardless of which blade was chosen. James was a connoisseur of knives. He tested each blade for balance, keenness of edge, and resiliency. But Black's knife had a guard between the handle and the blade. In addition, it was double-edged along the length of the curve near the end of the blade to the point. This innovation appealed to Bowie, and he chose Black's pattern over his own. According to Mrs. R. G. Halter of the Alamo Museum, the knife Bowie accepted was fourteen inches long, single-edged to the curve of the point, where both sides had been keened to a razor edge. The curve started about two and a half inches from the point and the blade was one and seven-eighths inches wide in breadth. The hilt of the knife was protected by a two pronged cross-guard, with overall length about three inches. The handle was made of seasoned black walnut.

Shortly after Bowie returned to Texas with his new purchase, he was attacked by three ruffians who had been hired for the express purpose of killing him.[7] The three would-be assassins quickly found out they had made a terrible mistake in accepting the assignment. Instead of succumbing to the unexpected assault, Bowie used his new knife with such efficiency that he managed to kill all of his attackers. This, according to Raymond Thorp in his *Bowie Knife,* was the battle that gave to Bowie and his knife such undying fame.

Word of Bowie's disposal of the three would-be murderers soon spread. From then on, when ordering a knife from Black, many customers would order it to be made "like Bowie's." Other purchasers would exclaim, "Make me a Bowie knife." Hence, the weapon acquired its famous name.

Black's happy life soon went into reverse. In the sketch Jones wrote, Anne Black died around 1837 or 1838. William Shaw, Jones continued, still heartily disliked his son-in-law for marrying his daughter against his wishes and then successfully competing against him. He was determined to extract his revenge.

Black was alone at home one day in the summer of 1839, in very poor physical condition as he was suffering from the effects of a prolonged fever. Suddenly, his father-in-law entered the house and without warning struck him over the head several times with a heavy stick. He continued his unwarranted attack and would probably have killed Black if the latter's dog, hearing the commotion, hadn't rushed to his master's defense. The dog jumped and seized Shaw by the throat and almost killed him before losing his hold, enabling the attacker to escape. The blows to the head he received resulted in inflamation in Black's eyes, which caused him to virtually go blind.

As soon as Black recovered from his illness and his beating, he started for Philadelphia to consult surgeons about his eyes. While on a steamboat, someone persuaded him to stop in Cincinnati to consult a physician who was supposed to be a fine eye doctor. The highly recommended doctor proved to be a quack, so Black continued his journey to Philadelphia and stayed there for around a year, being treated by various doctors all to no avail. He then returned home by way of New Orleans to consult with the celebrated Dr. Stone who, after a thorough examination, told him his eyesight was gone forever.

When Black returned to his home he found he had been struck another hard blow, but this one to his pocketbook. In his absence, somehow his unprincipled father-in-law had managed to liquidate all of his property and convert the proceeds to his name. Black was now around forty years of age, blind, homeless, and penniless.

The unfortunate man still had friends, and among them were two brothers named Jacob and John Buzzard. These two gentlemen owned a plantation in Lafayette County (now Miller), Arkansas, which was situated on a high bluff on Red River. Sympathizing with his plight, the brothers invited Black to make his home with them. He accepted and lived with them for about two years.

Sometime during 1842, Black heard about a Dr. Isaac N. Jones, who had recently moved to Washington, Arkansas, from Bowie County, Texas. Dr. Jones was rapidly achieving an excellent reputation as a skilled physician and surgeon, and Black was hopeful that the doctor could perhaps enable him to regain some of his sight. He requested the Buzzard brothers to send him to Washington for a consultation with the highly respected medical man, and they did.

Dr. Jones gave Black a thorough examination of his eyes, and then told him there was a slight possibility the sight in the right eye could be restored; that of the left eye, he stated, was forever lost. To recover any sight in his right eye it would be necessary for Black to move back to Washington, where he could be treated constantly. Black replied that was impossible, as he was utterly destitute and would have to remain with his friends.

"No, no," replied Dr. Jones. "You can come and live with me and my family and I will trust to the future for any compensation."

Daniel Webster Jones was the son of Dr. Isaac Jones and, according to him, "at the time James Black came to live with us, I was an infant just beginning to prattle. My father used his best skill in an effort to restore Black's sight, but all to no avail. Being honest, he told his patient that it would be futile to torture him with further treatments. 'But,' said my father, 'you need have no fears. You shall live with us always.'" The doctor then told Black that he would be sufficiently compensated if he would see after and advise his four young boys while he was away from home attending to his many patients.

Dr. Jones died on February 11, 1858, after being killed by the explosion of a steam boiler on his plantation. By common consent, Black remained with the family. After the death of Mrs. Jones in January 1867, the future governor took Black to live in his house in Washington. There Black stayed until he died on June 22, 1872. Jones had nothing but fond memories of Black:

> My earliest recollections are connected with him. His kindness and fatherly advice to me and my brothers endeared him to us all, and my father felt that he was sufficiently compensated by the manner in which he executed the trust of looking after us. He was greatly attached to us all, but especially

to my eldest brother, Isaac, and after Isaac's death at the age of fourteen, the old man transferred his affection to me. While he lived in my father's house, the doctor's office was his room, and I slept there frequently, read to him, and led him about the premises.[8]

Jones related that Black had an extraordinary memory, and when the older settlers engaged in a controversy concerning some happenings of earlier days, the blind man was selected as referee. Jones continued in his saga:

Time and time again, when I was a boy, he would say to me that notwithstanding his great misfortune, God had blessed him by giving him a good home among friends, and that one day, when I had reached maturity, he would disclose to me his secret of tempering steel. I did not press him as to this, although naturally very curious, and it was not until my mother's death, when he moved into my home, that it seemed he was getting ready to trust me with his secret.

On May 1, 1870, which was his seventieth birthday, Mr. Black told me that since, in the ordinary course of nature he would not expect to live much longer, he had decided that the time had arrived. He stated that I was old enough and sufficiently well acquainted with the affairs of the world to properly utilize the secret, and that if I would procure pen, ink and paper, he would communicate his knowledge to me.

I lost no time in bringing the materials to him. After sitting in silence for awhile, he said: "In the first place" — and then stopped and began rubbing his brow with the fingers of his right hand.

He continued in this way for some minutes, as if trying to reconstruct something in his mind, and then, still rubbing his brow, said: "Go away and come back in an hour."

I did so, but remained close to the open door where I could see him, and not for one moment did he take his fingers from his brow, or change his position.

At the expiration of the hour I went in and spoke to him. Without a perceptible movement he said: "Go out again, and come back in an hour's time." This I did, and the same process was again repeated, and again. When I came to him at the end of the third hour Mr. Black burst into tears, saying "My God! It is all gone from me! All these years I have accepted the kindness of these good people in the belief that I could partly repay it with this, my only legacy. Daniel, there are ten or twelve processes through which I put my knives — but I cannot now remember even one of them. A few hours ago, when I told you to get the writing materials, everything was fresh in my mind. Now it has flown. I have put it off too long."

I looked at Mr. Black in awe and wonder. His forehead was raw and bleeding, where the skin and flesh had been rubbed off by his fingers. His sightless eyes were filled with tears, and his face expressed utter grief and despair. I could only say: "Never mind, Mr. Black. It is all in the wisdom of God. He knows best; and undoubtedly He had His reasons for allowing the secret of the Bowie Knife to remain with you."

The inventor of the Bowie Knife lived with me slightly more than two years following this scene — but from that moment on he was a hopeless imbecile. The struggle to impart the secret had destroyed his mind. God gave him the secret for His own purposes, but was unwilling for him to impart it to others.

When James Black died, he was buried in an old cemetery on the northern edge of Washington, Arkansas.[9]

There might have been and still might be controversy as to who really invented the Bowie knife and gave the blade its name. The *Washington Telegraph* of Hempstead County, Arkansas, certainly had no qualms in deciding who had the honors. In an article dated December 8, 1841, headed "The Bowie Knife," the publication stated that "the far-famed deadly instrument had its origin, we believe in Hempstead County. The first knife of the kind was made in this place, by Mr. James H. Black, for a man named James Bowie, who was killed at the Alamo, Texas, and hence it is sometimes called the Black knife, sometimes the Bowie knife." The article several times refers to the "Bowie" knife, and later on remarks "while on this subject we cannot forbear mentioning the sad dispensation with which Mr. James H. Black, the inventor of this knife, has been visited. Several years since he lost his eyesight."

CHAPTER 8

More About
James Black

Former Governor Daniel Webster Jones told the story of James Black in good faith, no doubt, and as the latter related it to him. It must be remembered, however, that the tale Black told concerned events that had transpired many years previously. Also, he was a man of advanced years, broken in health and very possibly embittered at the way he had been treated by life. Perhaps unconsciously, Black colored the facts somewhat as there are some discrepancies in the story he told, and it is possible that all the facts pertaining to Black vs. Shaw were not presented. Actual records show that Shaw, his father-in-law, was not the complete villain he had been portrayed by the younger man.

A fact that Black didn't tell Jones (or if he did the latter forgot to relate it in his story) was that it was William Shaw who put a notice of the marriage of his daughter to Black on June 29, 1828, in the Washington *Gazette*. The pretty Anne was some eight years younger than her husband, having been born in Tennessee in 1808.

On October 6, 1835, the Arkansas *Gazette* carried a notice that "Mrs. Anne Black, aged twenty-seven years, died, leaving a disconsolate husband, five children, and numerous connections and friends to deplore her premature death." The Jones article giving the death of Anne Black as 1837 or 1838 was obviously in error, but did Jones' memory play him false, or was it the faulty memory of Black?

Black was a well-respected man in his community, and was active in other pursuits besides only blacksmithing. The records of Hempstead County Court show that he served on jury duty and received a dollar per day for his services. He was liked, and possibly had some political influence, as he held several appointive positions in the county.

In July 1828, shortly after being married, Black was appointed overseer of the road leading from Washington to the eastern boundary of Saline township.[1] For the period of 1826–1832, he and three other men were appointed patrols for Ozan township with the requirement they patrol at least twelve hours in each month. County records also show that on October 12, 1832, Black was apppointed deputy jailer in and for Hempstead County.[2]

The Jones article avers that it was during the summer of 1839 that Shaw, while Black was at home suffering from the effects of a protracted fever, entered the latter's home and beat him so severely with a stick that it eventually resulted in the loss of his eyesight. There are no county records of any such beating, and it is possible Black's fever caused his blindness.

The records of Hempstead County Circuit Court show that three years before this alleged assault—on May 11, 1836, to be precise—William Shaw appeared before the court. In his appearance he exhibited information in writing stating that, among other things, Black was subject to spells of insanity and was incapable of prudently managing his affairs.

The court apparently believed the evidence Shaw presented, as they appointed him guardian of his son-in-law with the stipulation he present a bond in the amount of $4,000. (It seems that at that time Black had an estate of a probable value of $2,000.) Shaw made bond for that sum and was paid $10 per month by the court for his guardianship. Shaw remained as the guardian of Black until October 6, 1839.

On October 25, 1841, the Probate Court of Hempstead County gave custody of the five children of James and Anne Black to Shaw. The four sons were to be bound to him as apprentices until they reached the age of twenty-one, while the daughter, Sarah Jane, was bound as apprentice until she was eighteen.

The years passed by until 1844. During the April term of that year, the Hempstead County Court declared Black to be a pauper as he was blind and unable to support himself and was without means or estate to do the same. Consequently, they appointed Simon T. Sanders, as commissioner of the county, to contact some suitable person to support, maintain, and clothe James

Black on the best terms he could get. During the July term of the court, Sanders reported that Dr. Isaac N. Jones was willing to board, lodge, and wash for the said James Black for $10 per month.

It seems that somewhere along the line a John B. Sandefur was appointed commissioner to look after Black, as the court records show that during the July term of 1848 he was discharged from that post. In his stead, one John Gabbart was named to take care of the blind man and was paid quarterly installments of $100 for doing so.

As late as October 1870, the Citizens for the Relief of James Black petitioned the court, urging that the county treasurer and citizens pay to have Black cared for. The court agreed, and renewed the payments every two months until Black died in 1872.[3]

If William Shaw was the ogre Daniel Webster Jones presented him to be in his article in the Arkansas *Gazette,* it certainly seems odd that he would be appointed the guardian of his son-in-law, and later on be given custody of his five grandchildren. He moved to Texas in 1850, and in that year still had custody of two of his grandchildren—James and John Culbert Black.

A hypothesis of the alleged beating of Black by Shaw could be explained as follows: Perhaps Black, grieved at the loss of his beloved wife, had fits of depression and even perhaps temporary insanity. It could have been during one of these moments that Shaw called upon Black and had to subdue him as the latter, during his depressed rage, tried to attack Shaw with a heavy stick. Such is merely hypothesis, but possible.

The James Black story is a strange story indeed, and if the skilled blacksmith ever knew the secret of tempering steel as was credited to the ancient Damascans, the secret lies buried with him.

The question still remains: Did Black, or did he not, make the first Bowie knife as we know it today—a knife with a curved guard between the handle and the blade, and the blade curved on the end?

So ends the saga of James Black.

CHAPTER 9

The Bowie
Knife Craze

After the Battle of the Sandbar, and particularly after Bowie used his knife so successfully to defend himself against the three hired would-be assassins (this particular fight will be examined in more detail in a later chapter), the popularity of the Bowie knife grew so fast that the craze to own one became insatiable. Many craftsmen and manufacturers made their version of the weapon. Not only that, but Bowie knife schools, where one could learn the art of cut, thrust, and parry, were formed in all the major cities of the Southwest, from St. Louis to New Orleans.[1]

The proper stance for a right-handed knife fighter was as follows: knife in hand, left foot slightly forward, head set well back. The knife is usually held sidewise in the hand, thumb alongside the blade, just beyond the guard. The fighter is now in position to deliver a slashing, sidewise blow, or a ripping uppercut. The head is never a target for the professional knife fighter; his possible bullseye is encompassed in that space between the throat and hips.[2]

Lucy Leigh Bowie, in her article, stated that James Bowie's manner of grasping the Bowie knife was considered peculiar; he held it as one would a sword, and once beyond the opponent's guard, the thrust was deadly.[3]

Noah Smithwick had known James Bowie since 1828, shortly after the latter first arrived to settle permanently in Texas, and later fought with him at the Battle of Concepción. According to Smithwick, the knife Bowie used at the sandbar

> was an ordinary affair with a plain wooden handle, but when
> Bowie recovered from his wounds he had the precious blade

polished and set into an ivory handle mounted with silver; the scabbard also being silver mounted. Not wishing to degrade it by ordinary use, he brought the knife to me in San Felipe to have a duplicate made. The blade was about ten inches long and two broad at the widest part. When it became known that I was making a genuine Bowie knife, there was a great demand for them, so I cut a pattern and started a factory, my jobs bringing all the way from $5.00 to $20.00, according to finish.[4]

Smithwick was only one of many wanting to cash in on the craze to own a Bowie knife. Bowie's fame had quickly spread to England, and by the early 1830s a flood of British-made Bowies began arriving on the American market. Some of the British-made Bowies came from London and Birmingham, but the vast majority were produced by various manufacturers in Sheffield, England, with virtually the entire Sheffield production being shipped to America.[5] And all across the United States, from the South to New York to San Francisco, American craftsmen were supplying the demand for the knives.

Capt. Rees Fitzpatrick had lived in Baton Rouge, Louisiana, prior to moving to Natchez, Mississippi. An expert craftsman in silver and gold,[6] he was an expert gunsmith and made many presentation swords. He also, at Gen. Sam Houston's suggestion, made the first Bowie bayonets.[7] Fitzpatrick made Bowie knives of such excellent quality that they were said to be far superior to the many millions being made in England in that his blades were elastic while the latter, with blades hardened in order to present a high polish, were hardly stronger than pot metal. A knife Fitzpatrick made for a Dr. L. P. Blackburn of Mississippi was supposedly so elastic that it quivered at being touched, and bore "an unsurpassed edge, keen as the lightning flash."[8]

The "Philadelphia cutler" Lucy Leigh Bowie referred to was one Henry Schively, who lived at 75 Chestnut Street in the late 1820s and early 1830s. Later, in the late 1830s, he moved to 64 South 8th Street and worked there before disappearing from the listings.

Schively, a prominent cutler and surgeons instrument maker, made a number of Bowie knives, at least one for Rezin Bowie. Rezin had a number of knives made in his lifetime, and from time to time would present them to friends. One knife bore the mark of Henry Schively on the blade, and the initials "R. P. B."

engraved in script letters on the pommel. The knife has no guard handle, is single-edged, and has no curved point on the end. The blade is ten and one-fourth inches. In other words, it is similar to the ordinary kitchen knife used today, and certainly fits Rezin's description of the knife he gave his brother.

Engraved on the silver sheath are the words "Presented to Jesse Perkins by R. P. Bowie – 1831." Perkins was a resident of Natchez, and served under the command of Jefferson Davis with the lst Mississippi Rifles during the Mexican War.[9] This knife, since 1918, has been on display in the State Historical Museum, Department of Archives and History, Jackson, Mississippi.

Among the knives Rezin Pleasant Bowie gave to friends was one he presented to Henry Waller Fowler, captain of the 2nd U.S. Dragoons. The length of the blade is nine and one-fourth inches, with an overall length of fourteen and one-eighth inches, and is very similar to the Schively knife described above. Manufactured by Daniel Searles, gunsmith, blacksmith, and knife-maker of Baton Rouge, Louisiana, the handle is made of checkered ebony. A gold plate inlaid in the blade's back is inscribed "Searles. Baton Rouge, La.," while the sheath's coin silver throat bears the phrase "R. P. Bowie to H. W. Fowler, U.S.D."

Supposedly, this knife was used by James Bowie during the attack on the Alamo. After Bowie was killed, the knife was secreted by an Indian woman who had been nursing him while the Alamo was under siege. According to the story, the woman later gave the knife to Rezin. There is no date on the knife as to when Rezin presented it to his friend Fowler, but inasmuch as Rezin died in 1841, the presentation was made during the years 1836 to 1841.

This particular knife passed through a series of hands and was eventually put up for auction in 1902, when it was purchased by Gen. Washington Bowie, Jr., of Baltimore. In 1951 the knife was donated to the Daughters of the Republic of Texas by Lt. Col. Richard T. Bowie, son of the deceased Gen. Washington Bowie, Jr., and is today on display at the Alamo Museum in San Antonio, Texas.

Governor E. D. White of Louisiana was the recipient of a Bowie knife given by Rezin, as was a Mr. Stafford of Alexandria. One was also given to the famous nineteenth-century American actor Edwin Forrest, who was a friend of both James and Rezin until James' death in 1836 and Rezin's in 1841.

A native of Philadelphia, Forrest was a handsome man with a fine physique and was enormously popular in both the United States and England. He played the South many times and in the spring of 1829 appeared in New Orleans, Natchez, and other cities while starring in *Hamlet, King Lear,* and other classics. It was said that the knife Forrest used in the stage play *Matamora* was the original Bowie knife, presented to him by Bowie when Forrest visited him at his plantation.

Later on, Forrest built a magnificent home in Philadelphia. An avid collector of rare manuscripts, antiques, works of art, and memorabilia of his life on the stage, he had a library filled with all of those items. Separate from the library, in an art gallery or another room, he had a large weapons case filled with weapons which were meaningful to him. Among them was a Bowie knife, Forrest proudly told all, that had been given him by his friend James Bowie. Several months after Forrest died in 1872, the library in the mansion was destroyed by fire, and the books, works of art, rare manuscripts, and other memorabilia were destroyed. The Bowie knife, being in another room, was saved. In 1989 or 1990 the Bowie knife came into the possession of William R. Williamson of California, a noted knife collector.

Edwin Forrest possessed at least one other Bowie knife, one made by John D. Chevalier, a cutler and surgical and dental instrument maker in New York. A knife Forrest presented to Joseph Davis bears the inscription "Presented by Edwin Forrest, Esq., to Joseph Davis Feb. 12th, 1849" and was a Cavalier Bowie. The knife, with a blade which is ten and one-fourth inches long, has a sharp false edge with a handle of one piece stag. The sheath has a brass throat and tip.

And what happened to Bowie's personal knife that he used to defend himself at the Alamo? During his lifetime he owned several knives, and it is conceivable he had more than one on his person when the Alamo was stormed.

As previously mentioned, one knife supposedly owned by Bowie was smuggled out of the Alamo by an Indian woman. There is at least one other Bowie knife that has surfaced that many people think may have been used by Bowie during the defense of the Alamo. This particular weapon has a thick blade more than eight inches long and more than an inch and a half wide. The smooth, hardwood handle is topped by a heavy iron knob, which adds another five inches to the overall length. The handle and blade are separated by a guard. On the front of the blade the name "J. Bowie" is etched, as is the acorn symbol of James Black, the Arkansas blacksmith.

This particular weapon has an interesting story behind it. A young Mexican soldier serving with Santa Anna found the knife in the rubble after the fall of the Alamo, so the tale goes. The *vaquero* carried the knife for years on the Texas cattle range, and in 1890 gave the knife to James F. Moore to pay off a debt of $5. Moore eventually gave it to his son Elisha, who gave it to his son Bart in 1947. Later on, Bart carried the knife as a personal weapon when he served in Europe with the Air Force Security. Bart still owns the knife, which presently is kept in a bank vault.

An interesting question is what happened to the knife Bowie used at the sandbar that he had Noah Smithwick polish and set into an ivory handle mounted with silver? Or the duplicate he had Smithwick make with a blade ten inches in length and two inches wide? It goes without saying that any knife or knives used by James Bowie at the Alamo, and that could be authenticated as his personal property, would be of enormous value. Bart Moore, who lives in California, states that as far back as 1976 he was offered $50,000 for the knife he possesses, and claims tentative bids have recently been tendered as high as $3 million.

CHAPTER 10

In a New Home

A fter James Bowie had recovered from the wounds inflicted upon him at the sandbar, he decided to move to Texas. His brother John stated the reason for the move was that he felt he had not been well used or properly treated by some of his political friends. Very likely James also had business reasons for leaving Louisiana, as the land speculation deals he had been involved in were now being challenged in the courts. Too, he was probably not pleased with the notoriety he had received for his part in the sandbar incident.

Before moving to Texas, however, James attended a dinner in New Orleans given by Stephen F. Austin in honor of President Andrew Jackson. Jackson was in the city as the guest of the State of Louisiana to celebrate the victory of the Battle of New Orleans in 1815 over the British, and the dinner was recorded as a "meeting of choice spirits." At this dinner Bowie revealed he had a knack for public speaking, as he gave an eloquent toast and oration in honor of the president.[1]

On several occasions in the past Bowie had visited Texas and liked what he saw, deciding the place was ripe for land speculation. Now it was to be his home. In the early months of 1828 he decided to visit there and take a look around.

Unlike the majority of colonists, who had settled in the eastern portion of the state, Bowie rode past the Brazos River until he reached San Antonio de Bexar. Bexar, as the town was popularly called, was deep into the interior and in the "Spanish" country, as it was largely settled by Mexicans. Bowie decided to make the town his headquarters.

With Bowie's good looks and manly physique, his charm and pleasing personality, he always found it easy to make influential friends. It wasn't long before he had met most of the important men in San Antonio. Among these was Don Juan Martin de Veramendi, who was soon to become vice-governor of the dual state of Coahuila-Texas.

Veramendi and his wife, Dona Maria Josefa Navarro de Veramendi, were aristocrats of pure Spanish Castilian blood and their marriage had united two of the chief families of Spanish Texas. Among their children was the lovely Maria Ursula. The eldest of seven children, she had been baptized November 1, 1811, at the age of six days. Despite the difference in their ages, James was immediately attracted to the stunning girl.

In 1824 the Mexican government had adopted a new federal constitution. Among its provisions, it prohibited any religious faith other than Roman Catholicism. It had two other clauses that raised the hackles of the Anglos living in the state, and later on caused considerable friction between them and the Mexican government. One clause gave preference to Mexican citizens in the distribution of land, and another clause required the would-be colonist to appear before the local *ayuntamiento*, the municipal government, and swear allegiance to the Mexican constitution.[2]

Bowie was a shrewd individual, and he decided that if he wanted to acquire Mexican land—and preferably large quantities of it—it would be advantageous if he became a Roman Catholic. Consequently, he converted to that religion. Unfortunately, the existing San Fernando Church records do not list Bowie's baptism as they do his wedding. Neither do the baptismal records of the San Jose church, which Bowie later attended. It is possible, of course, that he was baptized elsewhere

Although he was in Texas, James was still engaged in land tract ventures in Louisiana. Conveyance records of Lafourche Parish show that several times in 1828 his brother Stephen, using a power-of-attorney given him by James, sold land tracts for his brother.[3]

While in Texas, Bowie devoted several months traveling around the state in a fruitless search for the fabled San Saba silver mines that were chronicled in old Spanish records.[4] Not finding the mines, he vowed never to give up his quest but to search for them another day.

In the spring of 1829 Bowie decided to visit his brother Rezin at the plantation near Helena, Arkansas, and his mother in Louisiana. His purpose was to persuade them to come back to Texas with him, at least temporarily. He needed Rezin's help in his business ventures, but more than that, he desired his help in searching for the lost silver mines of San Saba.

Although Bowie usually had money, his constant land speculations at times would leave him strapped for cash. It had happened sometime previously when he had been turned down for a loan by his enemy Norris Wright; consequently, a piece of property he owned had been foreclosed on. It had happened again, and on September 26, 1829, brother Stephen bought a land tract that had been "seized" from James by court action.

Helena was a small hamlet of some twenty cabins and six grog shops, on the eastern border of Arkansas, just across the river from Mississippi. It was in this hamlet that Bowie first met the well-known Sam Houston. Houston had been governor of Tennessee, but on April 16 had resigned from his position after a brief, unhappy marriage. Now he was on his way west to the Indian territory to live once more among his friends, the Cherokees.

The former governor was six years older than Bowie, and at 6'3 was two inches taller than the younger man. The two men struck up an immediate friendship as they had much in common. Both of them were outdoorsmen with powerful physiques—Houston was reputed to have a forty-eight-inch chest—and both were fearless and courageous, with strong personalities that enabled them to quickly make friends. Best of all, they were natural born leaders.

All of his life, Houston traveled in the company of first-class men. He was a shrewd judge of men's capabilities and character and took an instant liking to Bowie, who reciprocated the feeling. No doubt they visited one or more of the grog shops, and when they parted neither man realized that when they met again it would be under entirely different circumstances and that their lives would be entwined so dramatically in the birth of a new nation.

In early 1830 Bowie returned to Texas for good. Before leaving Louisiana, though, in a transaction taking place at Rezin's residence on January 15, he sold his interest in a plantation and thirty-four slaves to his brothers Stephen and Rezin.[5] Eight days later he gave Stephen his power-of-attorney before a parish judge in LaFayette Parish, Louisiana.

Bowie passed through Nacogdoches, Texas, on February 13. While there, he applied, as a single man, for one-fourth of a league of land on Galveston Island, stating that he had 109 "dependents" (interpreted as slaves). While there, he met Thomas F. McKinney, a prominent businessman, and from him secured a letter of recommendation to Stephen F. Austin, the empresario who had received permission from the Mexican authorities to bring colonists from the United States into Texas. James was in Nacogdoches so briefly that he didn't learn that the land he applied for had already been granted.

Given a choice as to where he wanted to settle his colonists, Austin had selected a beautiful site, watered by the Brazos, Guadalupe, Colorado, and San Antonio rivers, and named his capital San Felipe de Austin.

When Bowie arrived at the capital, he promptly sought out Austin and presented his letter of introduction. The letter read:

> Permit me to introduce to you Mr. James Bowie, a gentleman who stands highly esteemed by his acquaintances, and merits the attention particularly of the citizens of Texas as he is disposed to become a citizen of that country and will evidently be able to promote its general interests. I hope that you and Mr. Bowie may concur in sentiments and that you may facilitate his views.[6]

After presenting himself and his letter of introduction to Austin, Bowie mounted his horse once more and proceeded in a leisurely fashion eighty miles south to San Antonio. He found suitable lodgings on Soledad Street and after looking the town over, decided to make San Antonio his permanent residence. John Bowie remarked that at this time, on his brother's permanent move to Texas, he had around $1,000 with him, which he invested in lands.[7]

Later that year, on August 14, Samuel Rhodes Fisher, who later became secretary of the navy under the presidency of Sam

Houston in the Republic of Texas,[8] wrote Austin that "The most valuable emigrant you have ever had is James Bowie. I consider him of the best order of men."[9]

On May 1, 1718, the Mission San Antonio de Valero was established in San Antonio. The mission was named in honor of the Marquis of Valero, the viceroy of Mexico, and for the San Antonio River that flowed gently through the area. Four days later, on May 5, a tiny village named Villa de Bexar was founded. The same day a fort, Presidio de San Antonio de Bexar, was founded. Both were founded near San Pedro Springs, and both were named in honor of the Duke of Bexar, the viceroy's brother and one of Spain's heroes. The presidio was established to protect the settlement from the Indians that roamed the area, primarily the fierce Apaches and Comanches.

On March 9, 1731, sixteen families consisting of fifty-six people arrived in San Antonio de Bexar from the Canary Islands. Theirs was the first civil settlement in Texas, established by decree of the King of Spain in an effort to hold the Texas frontier. The Spanish viceroy named the little settlement Villa de San Fernando, in honor of the heir to the throne of Spain. The islanders promptly laid out the townsite with a plaza and locations for government offices, and for their church, the San Fernando Cathedral.

In 1830, when Bowie settled permanently in Bexar, as it was commonly called then, the town had a population of around 2,500. During the days of Spanish rule the town had been an important center of culture, but after Mexico won its independence from the parent nation, it became just another frontier outpost and in the past eight years the town had lost over half of its population. Yet, Bexar still had a noticeable Spanish charm.

The majority of the population at that time was Mexican, as were virtually all of the leading businessmen and social figures in the community. James, with his charm and fluency in Spanish, quickly established friendships with many prominent Mexicans who later were sympathetic to the Anglo cause, such as Francisco Ruiz, Placedo Benavides, Jose Cassiano, and Jose Antonio Navarro, nephew of Francisco Ruiz and brother-in-law of Don Juan Martin de Veramendi. Ruiz and Navarro later became the only two native-born Texans to sign the Texas Declaration of Independence.

Veramendi had become tax collector and *alcalde* (mayor) of Bexar. In 1832 he would become governor of the dual state of Coahuila–Texas. His daughter Ursula, now eighteen, was lovelier than ever. James also became good friends and companion-in-arms with Caiaphas K. Ham, an Anglo who remarked of Bowie: "He was a true, constant and generous friend . . . He was a foe no one dared to undervalue, and many feared . . . he was a recognized leader of men."

Bowie loved San Antonio and the easy life the Mexicans led with their friendliness and courtesy, and his knowledge of Spanish helped him form many new friendships within the city. He had thought of Ursula many times since he first met her, and with the couple's renewed acquaintance he quickly found he was becoming more and more fascinated with the lovely girl. With the consent of the Veramendi family, it wasn't long before he was paying court to her.

Although the Texas Rangers were not formally organized until October 17, 1835,[10] the organization was informally organized as early as 1823 when Austin, using the authority granted him by the Mexican government, employed on his own account and at his own expense ten men to serve as Rangers. Later on, he raised thirty men whose primary duties were to chase Indians.[11]

Bowie's leadership qualities were quickly recognized in his new home, and in 1830 a group of Rangers in San Antonio elected him as their colonel. During the next five years he, as commander of his volunteers, engaged in numerous skirmishes with hostile Indians.

Knowing that it would help him in his capacity as a businessman, Bowie petitioned the Mexican government to grant him citizenship. If granted, he promised he would build wool and cotton mills in the Coahuila portion of the dual state. On September 30, 1830, citizenship was granted to him under Decree No. 159, which reads as follows:

His excellency, the Governor of the State, has been pleased to forward the following decree:

The Governor of the State of Coahuila and Texas to all its inhabitants, Know Ye: That the congress of the said state has decreed the following:

Decree No. 159. The Constitutional Congress of the free,

independent and sovereign State of Coahuila and Texas decrees the following:

A letter of citizenship is hereby granted to the foreigner, James Bowie, providing he establishes the wool and cotton mills which he offers to establish in the state.

The Governor of the State will be guided by this decree, and for its compliance therewith he shall have it printed, published, and distributed. Issued in the City of Leona Vicario on September 30, 1830. Ramon Garcia Rojas, Congressional Chairman; Mariano Garcia, Congressional Secretary; Vicente Valdez, Congressional Secretary, pro-tem.

Wherefore, I command this decree to be printed, published and circulated, and command proper obedience thereto.

Leona Vicario,
October 5, 1830
Rafael Eca y Muzquis   Santiago del Valle
                                                   Secretary

Bowie quickly honored his promise. He and Veramendi went into partnership and set up their cotton and wool mills at Saltillo, Coahuila. After the mills were set up, however, he left the operation of them to Veramendi, who subsequently established a residence at Saltillo in addition to the one he already had at Bexar. This was convenient to him because as one of the leading political figures in Coahuila–Texas, he frequently had to be in Mexico on political business; in addition, the Veramendi family also had a summer home in Monclova.

James promptly took advantage of his new Mexican citizenship, which gave him the right to buy up to eleven leagues of public land (a league being 4,428.4 acres) at from $100 to $250 per league. This purchase of land was a right that was withheld from colonists, unless they were Mexican citizens.

Once more Bowie indulged in land speculation, and when he returned to Texas he returned with titles, or options on titles, for fifteen or sixteen eleven-league grants that he had induced Mexican citizens to apply for and turn over to him. These grants totaled around 700,000 acres and represented a large amount of land for a speculator.

In addition to the leagues he bought, he also purchased headrights in all the empresario grants. His method, which some say he originated, was to induce a settler to apply for a grant, then buy it from him. Sometimes cash was paid, but another method also frequently employed was described by an 1834 traveler as follows:

> When an emigrant arrives in the country, he is met by a land speculator, who tells him he knows of a good location, and if he will claim and settle on it, he shall have one-half of the league for nothing. The land is entered at the land office in the emigrant's name, the speculator pays the fees, and takes a deed of one-half from the emigrant. This is not the worst kind of speculation in the world . . . The emigrant, at least, seems to have no cause for complaint. He gets twenty-three hundred acres of land, as much as he can ever cultivate, and pays nothing at all for it.[12]

As late as 1835 Bowie continued with his land speculation, and at one time was associated with one John T. Mason, a land agent. During the years 1834 and 1835, the Mexican government passed various laws that put an end to such speculation, so Bowie and most of the others engaged in the practice disposed of their holdings.

Bowie's growing fondness for Ursula had grown into love and it was reciprocated. He proposed, was accepted, and asked Veramendi for his daughter's hand in marriage. Permission was readily granted as Veramendi was extremely fond of his prospective son-in-law — he liked Anglos and was sympathetic to their cause — and the engagement was announced. On April 22, 1831, James signed a dowry contract.

James Bowie's powerful personality, and the effect he had on people, is indicated in his engagement to Ursula de Veramendi and his ready acceptance by her parents of him. On one side were the Veramendis, aristocrats of pure Spanish Castilian blood, and a wealthy family who held power socially, economically, and politically. Bowie, on the other hand, was a foreigner with little formal education. Essentially he was an adventurer prone to notoriety, and surely the news of the sandbar duel and Bowie's participation in it had penetrated to Bexar.

High-born, wealthy Mexican families have always been cautious as to whom they would let court their daughters. Ursula was beautiful and had wealthy parents. That in itself was a combination that would draw many suitors of her own race; yet, the

Veramendis were very fond of James and placed no obstacle in his way in the courtship of their daughter.

Very little is known of the love life of Bowie until his romance with Ursula. While living in Louisiana he is reported to have had hectic affairs with Judalon de Bornay, a beautiful, high-born Creole maid of New Orleans; Catherine Villars, a quadroon mistress of Jean Lafitte; and Sibil Cade, a rural Cajun swamp girl.[13] He had been engaged to Cecilia Wells, sister of the Wells brothers with whom he had been associated with in the sandbar encounter, but she died of pneumonia two weeks before the day set for the wedding.[14]

In his early manhood James had admired a beautiful young woman named Martha Gibson, who was from the Natchez area. It seems Martha looked with favor upon James, but on a visit to friends in New Orleans, she developed yellow fever and died.[15]

There was also a Miss Mentjo of New Orleans. A descendant of a long line of noble ancestors, she was smitten with Bowie but her family opposed the match on the grounds he was beneath her. They urged her to marry a count, but she remained firm in her desire to marry Bowie. Since neither she nor her parents would concede to the other, she finally received her parents' permission to enter a convent in France, where she had been educated. She entered the convent as a novice, and eventually took the veil.[16]

CHAPTER 11

Wedding Bells
and a Search
for Silver

T he wedding banns between Ursula and James were published three times, on April 11, 17, and 24, 1831.[1] Prelimi-
nary to the wedding, on April 22, James appeared before
Jose Maria Salina, the *alcalde* of San Antonio, and signed a dowry
contract. In the contract he promised to pay Ursula, within two
years of the marriage, $15,000 in cash or property of that value.

A listing of his assets revealed 60,000 arpents of land in Arkansas, at fifty cents per acre, for a total of $30,000; three notes
payable in the United States worth $97,800; and 15,000 arpents
of land on the Red River and the Washita in the state of Louisiana. At an estimation of $5 per arpent, these lands totaled
$75,000. There was also an amount in the hands of Angus McNeill
of $20,000 for the purchase of machinery and utensils in Boston
for the factory of cotton and wool. All of these assets totaled
$222,800, and in addition there were "various valuable Chattles,
lands and contracts entered into in this country which for the
present cannot be valued."

There being no notary public in San Antonio at that time,
the document was signed in the presence of Jose de la Garza, Jose
Balmaseda and Jose Cardenas, and witnessed by Jose Francisco
Floris and Janacio Arochas.[2] On the last page of the dowry contract is inscribed: "Court fees, 22 reales & no more."[3]

The sum of almost $223,000 that Bowie claimed was an enor-
mous amount of money for that time, but little of it was in hard
cash or in tangible land holding authentic titles. Possibly the
amount of $20,000 in the hands of Angus McNeill was in cash; if
so, it was the only claimed asset of Bowie that was indeed in cash.

He also neglected to mention that titles he claimed to land in
Arkansas were forged, and that notes on fraudulent sales were
not collectible.

On April 25, 1831, Maria Ursula de Veramendi, daughter of
the vice-governor of Coahuila–Texas and the goddaughter of
General Santa Anna, was married to James Bowie. A well-penned,
stately record of the ceremony may still be seen in the *Second Book
of Marriages* of the old San Fernando Cathedral in San Antonio,
where the ceremony was performed. Translated from Spanish
into English it reads:

> In the City of San Fernando de Bexar on the 25th day of
> April, 1831, I, the priest Don Refugio de la Garza, pastor of
> this city, having performed the investigation prescribed by the
> Canon Law, published the banns on three consecutive feast days
> — "Inter Missarund" during the high mass to wit, on the 11th,
> 17th, and 24th of said month, and having found no canonical
> impediment even after the lapse of 24 hours from the last
> publication of the banns, I married and blessed at the nuptial
> mass — "In Facie Ecclesiae" — publicly in the Church Don
> Santiago Bowie, a native of Louisiana of North America,
> legitimate son of Raymond Bowie and Albina Yons, and Miss
> Ursula de Veramendi, legitimate daughter of Don Juan Martin
> Veramendi and Dona Josefa Navarro. Their parents stood as
> sponsors, and Don Jose Angel Navarro and Don Juan Francisco
> as witnesses. In witness whereof I have hereinto affixed my
> signature.
>
> Refugio de la Garza[4]

The beautiful bride was nineteen and the groom was thirty-
five, although he gave his age as thirty.[5] Now that Bowie was a
married man, he received a headright league of land and seems
to have received a certificate for a labor of land (177 acres) that
was not patented until long after his death.[6]

Following the marriage, Bowie made a note to Josefa Ruiz
Navarro, Ursula's grandmother on her mother's side, in the
amount of $750[7] and then borrowed $1,879 from his new father-
in-law—strange acts for a supposedly wealthy man. James and his
new bride then took a leisurely honeymoon trip by stagecoach
and schooner to New Orleans and Natchez to introduce Ursula
to his relatives and friends.

The trip was a huge success. The lovely Ursula captivated

everyone she met with her charm, graciousness, gentleness, and beauty. In New Orleans she was pronounced to be one of the most beautiful women of the South, and when the couple went abroad they were "the observed of all observers."[8] While in New Orleans the couple met John James Audubon, the great artist and naturalist, and it is said that the artist painted a portrait of the two of them.[9]

It wasn't only in New Orleans or Gonzales that Ursula won the hearts of admirers. Capt. William G. Hunt of Texas wrote: "I first met Colonel Bowie and his wife at a party given them on the Colorado on Christmas Day, 1831. Mrs. Bowie was a beautiful Castilian lady, and won all hearts by her sweet manners. Bowie was supremely happy with her, very devoted and more like a kind and tender lover than the terrible duelist he has *since* been represented to be."[10]

When the couple returned to San Antonio, they built a stone and adobe house on a plot of land Ursula's father had given them[11] near the San Jose Mission, which they attended. There they lived in happiness for a while, but then the couple moved into the home of Ursula's parents, known as the Veramendi Palace, Calle Soledad Street. The building served not only as the residence of the Veramendis, but was also the office of the vice-governor.[12]

Among the Veramendis, Bowie was completely at ease as he was accepted by the family, which also consisted of Ursula's sister and an adopted brother, as one of their own. In the home he was "treated as a son and furnished with money and supplies without limit. While without regular occupation, he hunted for mines and mountains of gold or silver. When he made trips east he lived like a man who had plenty of money." It was furnished by Governor Veramendi.[13]

During his marriage to Ursula, Bowie was probably the happiest he had ever been. He was extremely devoted to her, as she was to him, and she made him a perfect wife. Although young in years, she was wise, tactful, and immensely helpful in Bowie's never-ending business deals. She was particularly helpful in fending off various Mexicans who had given Bowie unsecured funds for investment, and would write him tactfully that "here they have another way of thinking." Whatever the problem, and as a token of her love, she would always close her letters: "Receive thou the heart of thy wife."[14]

There were two children born of the exceedingly happy union between James and Ursula. In an article of the *Houston Chronicle* dated May 4, 1924, it was reported that a daughter named Maria Elve was born to the Bowies on March 20, 1832. According to the International Genealogical Index of the Mormon Church, she was born April 18, 1832, and named Maria Josepha Elve. A second child, James Veramendi Bowie, was born in Monclova on July 18, 1833.[15]

Although Bowie was a very happily married man with an adoring wife and living with a family that considered him more of a son than a son-in-law, the state of marriage did not change the restless nature of this frontiersman. He still had to be where the action was. He was frequently gone for long absences, indulging in business deals, chasing Indians with the Rangers, or in his never-ending quest for the lost San Saba silver mines.

From the early days of Spanish colonization there had been reports of marvelously rich silver mines near the site of the old San Saba Mission, which, according to John Bowie, were 200 miles northwest of Bexar. The mines apparently were first operated by the Indians, then seized by the Spaniards, who kept operations going with Indian labor. Emperor Agustin de Iturbide was interested in operating the mines, but after his abdication on March 19, 1823, government interest in them fizzled out.[16]

The area swarmed with hostile Indians, chiefly the Comanches, Lipan Apaches, and Karankawas, and the operation of the mines by Mexicans was practically impossible without the aid of government troops. The Indians had had a taste of what life had been like under the Spaniards, and they were quite content to have nothing further to do with the white man. Indians of the Lipan Apache tribe repossessed the mines and were working it when Bowie first began making his search, and frequently Indians would appear in San Antonio wearing some silver. This intrigued Bowie.

On one of his trips to the Indian country, Bowie had met Xolic, chief of the Lipan Apaches. The chief had broken a leg, and James had successfully set it. Xolic was so pleased that he had Bowie made a member of the tribe.[17]

Bowie was intelligent enough to know he had to ingratiate himself with the Lipans if he expected their cooperation in finding the silver mines. He knew if he could get their permission to enter their country he could then devote most of his time and energy to seeking the mines, and not have to worry about suddenly finding an arrow in his back. He carefully cultivated Chief Xolic, who had forbidden any of his tribe to reveal the location of the mines on pain of death by torture. The old man was grateful to Bowie for setting his leg, and might have eventually revealed the secret. Unfortunately, he died and was succeeded by Tres Manos (Three Hands), who distrusted all white men completely.

Tres Manos is said to have angered Bowie by bluntly telling him of his distrust of white men, and warning him to stay out of Lipan Apache country. James had spent months hunting and fighting with the tribe, and he didn't appreciate suddenly being told by Tres Manos to leave the tribal lands. He had never told the Indians he was on the search for the mines, but he thought they had discovered that he was, in fact, searching for them. He also thought he knew their location, or perhaps he had actually seen the fabulous lode.

It is entirely possible that Bowie may have secured some maps once owned by Louis Juchereau de St. Denis. St. Denis was an early French-Canadian explorer who not only found the mine, but held the Indians off long enough to extract a fortune from it. He had built a large house for himself and his beautiful wife, who shared his lonely life with him. Eventually he was murdered by the Indians, but his wife managed to escape. She later remarried, and retired to Spain.[18]

In a November 1898 issue of the St. Louis *Globe-Democrat*, an article was written by a man who used the name "Brazos." Brazos certainly thought that Bowie had managed to get hold of some maps of the San Saba area, and his article described some of Bowie's early trips into the San Saba country:

> . . . By some means he [Bowie] had got possession of a lot of old maps of Western Texas, and upon many of these were marked places that had been abandoned for a hundred years . . . Possibly Colonel Bowie secured his old map through his wife . . . it is certain that he had not been very long married before he began to talk of recruiting an expedition in search for St. Denis's silver mine, and the old house, which, at that period, was in the very heart of the country of the terrible Comanches. At that time

the house was only a little more than a hundred years old, and there was not a white man in Texas who had ever seen it. Colonel Bowie knew that there was such a place on his old map, and he had heard many stories of the wonderful wealth that St. Denis had gathered in the mountains near the old house and he did not allow many days to pass before he found himself at the head of some twenty-five or thirty adventurers prowling about in the mountains of the Guadalupe, southwest of San Antonio. After searching for more than a week, Bowie himself discovered St. Denis's old log house . . . there was St. Denis's name and the date, 1714, carved on a rock.[19]

As Brazos related in his article, shortly after they discovered the St. Denis house, they were forced to seek refuge in it as they were suddenly attacked by a band of Comanches. The Indians besieged them for two weeks. Bowie lost more than half of his men, and the rest managed to escape under cover of a storm.

A number of years prior to 1900, Ranger Capt. A. J. Sowell discovered between the Dry Frio and the Frio rivers a shaft, and near it a rough circle of rocks that looked to have been made for fortification. He connected the shaft and rocks with an account that his father heard Bowie give in Gonzales about 1831. Bowie had said that while prospecting for gold and silver in the mountains west of San Antonio, he sunk a shaft where there were indications of silver. He had about thirty men with him and, anticipating attacks from Indians, they fortified their camp by piling up large rocks about a hundred yards from a spring of water.[20]

According to Caiaphas K. Ham, as related in the *Memoires of John Salmon Ford*, (1:87–112, in the Texas State Archives at Austin), Rezin Bowie had visited the San Saba mine previous to 1831 and had used his tomahawk in getting possession of some ore. He carried it to New Orleans to have it assayed, and it panned out rich. On December 2, 1831, James and his brother Rezin, accompanied by Ham, six other men, and two servant boys, set out on an expedition to find the old silver mine. About a day's journey from the old San Saba Mission and the nearby ruins of the San Luis de las Amarillas fortress, the party was attacked by 164 Tawakoni, Waco, and Caddo Indians.[21] The successful defense put up by the Bowie group was one of the most thrilling and courageous in the annals of Indian fighting in the Southwest.

The fight started around 8:00 A.M. and would last all day long.

The Indians, armed with rifles, began to start grass fires. The Bowie party camped for defense in a thicket near water, and used knives and sticks to dig up rocks to build a rudimentary fortification. Outnumbered by the Indians, and with the odds against them, at one point the Bowie party were so desperate they determined to huddle back to back and fire their last bit of ammunition, then fight with knives as long as a single man was left. When the Indians finally gave up the fight and the battle was over, the Bowie group had one man killed and three wounded. In addition, five of their horses had been killed and three more wounded.

Upon his return to San Antonio, on December 10, 1831, Bowie wrote a report of the expedition, in Spanish, to "The Political Chief of Bexar." Very likely the political chief was Veramendi, his father-in-law. Rezin, in 1832, had a Philadelphia newspaper publish an account of the encounter. Both versions agree fully on the essentials and differ only slightly in immaterial details.[22]

Although Bowie, in his report, stated that he saw twenty-one Indians fall dead, more may have fallen. A group of Comanches later rode into Bexar and came upon the Caddo war party at a ceremony mourning their brothers lost in the battle. The Comanches counted fifty corpses and thirty-five who were merely wounded.

Once more, Bowie had added to his fame as a fighting man.

James never gave up his search for the fabled mines, and in 1832 made another fruitless search for them. And through the years he still had contact with the Indians. In a letter dated August 3, 1835, he described a "tour through the Indian villages" of friendly Shawnees and Cherokees, made for the purpose of recruiting braves to fight hostile tribes engaged in killing and plundering Mexican and American settlers.

CHAPTER 12

The Personal Side of Bowie

Just what sort of man was this James Bowie, who was born on the frontier and lived all of his life on the southwestern frontier during very turbulent times? A man of little formal education, in addition to his native English he could speak, read, and write Spanish and French fluently.

Bowie was a shrewd and ambitious man with a lifelong desire to make money, and he became an astute businessman. From his early years he was self-employed, and although at times he worked with other men or in partnership with other men, he never had a boss.

Generally very courteous, Bowie was well liked by both men and women. In his early years, when he first left the swamps of Louisiana, he might have felt a youthful awkwardness in society; however, he improved himself so that ultimately he could feel at ease in the best business and social circles of New Orleans and Texas.

A complex man, Bowie was generally good-natured and easy to get along with, but woe betide the man who incurred his anger, as Maj. Norris Wright and many others found out. His good looks, his pleasing personality, and his winning ways and charm made it easy for him to quickly create friendships. In that portion of Spanish Texas that he eventually made his home, he was extremely well liked by the Mexicans — so much so, in fact, that his friendship with them proved a very helpful asset in Texas' War for Independence against Mexico.

According to John J. Bowie, James was "possessed of an open, frank disposition, with a rather good temper, unless aroused by some insult, when the displays of his anger were terrible . . . but he was never known to abuse a conquered enemy, or to impose upon the weak and defenseless. A man of very strong social feelings, he loved his friends with all the ardor of youth, and hated his enemies and their friends with all the rancor of the Indian."[1]

Beneath his cool, inflexible exterior was deep-seated kindness and generosity. Fearless, he championed the cause of any person in trouble, particularly the little man who was unable to defend himself. He had profound reverence for womanhood, and in his relationships with women he was princely.[2]

Bowie's consideration and courtesy toward women were well known. The great statesman Henry Clay first met Bowie in a stagecoach on the Cumberland Road in 1832, and was a witness to one such incident.

As Clay later told the story, he, Bowie, a William McGinley, an unknown stranger with a pipe, and a young girl were in the stagecoach. Bowie was muffled in a huge cloak and faced constantly out the window, apparently in deep thought. The unknown man, seated by the side of Clay, was smoking a pipe constantly and soon filled the coach with smoke. The young girl began to cough and courteously asked the pipe-smoker to please stop smoking, as she was becoming ill. The smoker rudely replied that "he had paid his fare, and would do as he pleased." McGinley, who later wrote an article about the occurrence, stated that "the words were no sooner out of his mouth that my seatmate sprang up, threw aside his cloak, and drew from the back of his neck a wicked looking knife, *the worst I had ever seen.* He quickly seized the smoker by the chin, and, snapping his head back, placed the blade of the knife at this throat, saying: I will give you just one minute to throw that thing out of the window! Needless to say this was done, upon which my seatmate resumed his place, and again pulled the greatcoat about his face."[3]

From that meeting, Henry Clay developed a warm regard for Bowie and often referred to him as "that fine gentleman and patriot," as well as "the greatest fighter in the Southwest."[4]

Far from a braggart, Bowie never talked about his exploits. On the contrary, he was smooth, polished, and rarely raised his voice. But this very coolness somehow made him seem, when aroused, all the more lethal, and he usually got his way. Caiaphas K. Ham, a good friend of his, related an incident illustrating this.

James was a member of the Mexican legislature in Monclova in 1835 when President Santa Anna ordered the arrest of all Americans in the legislature. Bowie and a few others escaped, riding hard into Texas. Upon his arrival at Nacogdoches he was called upon to go on a mission to Chief Bowles of the Cherokees. As his horse was exhausted from the long, rapid flight from Mexico, James asked his friend Sam Houston to lend him his fine horse. Houston declined, saying, "I have but one and I need him."

"I'm going to take him," said Bowie, and left the room.

Houston then queried Caiaphas Ham, who was with them: "Do you think it right for me to give up my horse to Bowie?" Ham replied, "Perhaps it might be proper under the circumstances."

"Damn him, let him take the horse."[5]

The incident did nothing to diminish Houston's great admiration for his friend.

Bowie had his faults, but one of his best traits of character was that he loyally stood by his friends, right or wrong. In return, he expected the same from his friends. There is a story told about him getting into a fracas once in San Antonio. A friend who was present and witnessed the incident failed to give James any support, and Bowie later called him to account for it.

"But James," the friend exclaimed, "you were in the wrong."

"I know that as well as you do," replied Bowie. "That's just why I needed a friend. If I had been in the right I would have had plenty of them."[6]

Capt. William Y. Lacey, who spent eight months in the wilderness with Bowie in 1834, examining lands on the Trinity, was of the impression that Bowie was a wealthy man. He described him as being a roving man — sometimes searching for mines, sometimes fighting Indians, sometimes speculating in lands — but always a gentleman from bottom to top. He was accommodating, kind, and always had plenty of money. Lacey also mentioned that during the entire period the men spent together, he never once heard Bowie use profane language or an indecent or vulgar word, and commented that James was a man of singular modesty.[7]

Willie Williamson, under date of September 1, 1830, and while in New Orleans, wrote an article in which he claimed never to have heard a word hinted against Bowie's moral character, and that in money matters James was exceedingly liberal when there was occasion to be liberal.[8]

Bowie was a friend of John James Audubon, a young exile from Santo Domingo whose father's estates had been confiscated in the Haitian rebellion. The young Frenchman had settled in New Orleans, and although his first love was painting birds, he also taught school and painted portraits in order to make a living.

One account has it that Bowie met Audubon by accident when the latter was starving in an attic bedroom. Bowie helped him financially by lending him money to get on his feet. Later on, Bowie was supposed to have fought a duel with a Creole dandy who had insulted his friend. A conflicting account said that he met Audubon while in New Orleans on his honeymoon with Ursula.

Bowie was always ready to go to the assistance of anyone in trouble, regardless of whether they were a friend or stranger, if he thought they were being mistreated. A story told about his magnanimity was related by the Reverend C. W. Smith, who was the first Methodist minister sent to Texas by the congregation.

The preacher had crossed the Mississippi River and was overtaken by a large man mounted on horseback and armed with a rifle, pistol, and knife. Finding that they were both on their way to Texas, they decided to ride together. The minister gave his name and business to the stranger, who did not reciprocate.

Soon after they crossed the border into Texas, they came to a small village. The preacher indicated that he would like to stop for the night and preach a sermon. The stranger agreed, and said he would round up a congregation.

The evening meeting was in the open air, and the preacher was surprised and pleased at the large attendance. The services started with several hymns, and the congregation joined in lustily. However, when the minister finally started his sermon, he was interrupted by several catcalls and obnoxious remarks. Suddenly, his riding companion came up to the platform and addressed the audience, telling them that the Reverend Smith had come a long way to preach his sermon and was going to deliver it. In addition, the audience was going to stop their noise so he could be heard.

At that moment a burly tough in the audience rose and hollered out: "And who are you, and where did you come from?"

"That is immaterial, but my name is James Bowie. I rode

from Mississippi with this man, and I intend for him to get a square deal."

When Bowie's name was mentioned the crowd became subdued and the rowdy quickly shut up. There were no more interruptions, and the minister proceeded with his sermon.[9]

Juan N. Seguin, a Mexican who was loyal to the Texas cause during the revolution, was one of Sam Houston's chief scouts. In a letter he once described Bowie as "being known among the Mexicans from Saltillo to Bexar, and that whether they loved or hated him depended upon whether they were for or against Texas, but that whether they liked him or not, they all knew that he was absolutely brave, and that they could depend upon his being fair to foe and loyal to friends."[10]

Even Santa Anna admired Bowie's bravery. After the fall of the Alamo, when the Mexican dictator was looking at the bodies of the slain Texans, at first he gave orders for Bowie to be buried, saying that he was too brave a man to be burned like a dog. However, the generous mood passed and he turned off with the command: *"Pues no es cosa, escade!"*

Bowie may have had his detractors, but no one ever questioned his bravery. During the many years he was colonel of his Rangers he won the confidence and loyalty of all his men. He was prudent but at times daring in his recklessness, and his kindness and fellowship among his men, together with his unvarying fairness to friend and foe, won him the nickname of "the Young Lion" among his men.[11]

In early 1832, Bowie commanded a small company into the Indian country seeking revenge for their attack upon him, his brother Rezin, and their party the previous December. The Indians had received information of his coming and fled as from a pestilence, referring to him as "a fighting devil." Bowie and his group rode for several hundred miles, but never saw an Indian.[12]

Among other men who gave Bowie accolades was John J. Linn, who, in his *Reminiscences of Fifty Years in Texas,* referred to Bowie as "high-toned, chivalrous Jim Bowie."[13] Ranger Capt. A. J. Sowell credited James with "being skillful in all games played with cards and said he often won large sums of money. He had no fear of anything."[14] In fact, it was Bowie's proficiency with cards and his coming to the defense of unknown people that involved him in several duels.

General J. E. Jefferson of Seguin, Texas, knew James in Natchez in 1829. He traveled with Bowie on steamboats and stopped with him at taverns. The general said that Bowie "stood high as a citizen and a gentleman; that he was of incorruptible integrity, never violating plighted faith; that he was not a professional gambler, though he and almost everyone in that section in those days played poker and other games."[15]

In 1836 Enrique Esparza was a young lad in San Antonio, and together with his father Gregorio, his mother, and three other Esparza children, was in the Alamo, where his father was killed fighting for the Texas cause. Many years later, while talking to some San Antonio schoolchildren, he told of an incident concerning Bowie's kindness:

> My mother sold beef, tamales and beans to the Texans. I helped her to carry the earthern jars full of food. It was a heavy task at times. One day when I was carrying a jar along the log that made a footbridge over the San Antonio River, I slipped and fell into the deep water. Senor Bowie jumped in and brought me out. I could swim from the time I was four years old. This day I think I struck the log in falling, as I was very bloody. I was very fond of Senor Bowie after this. Senor Bowie had no family. Why? Sr. Veramendi and her two children had died. He was a sad man.

Enrique Esparza had then gone on to tell how Bowie had wanted to send him to the United States to get a good education, and that he would pay all the bills. Enrique's father thanked James, but was opposed to the idea, explaining to Bowie that the Esparzas were just simple folk and not in his (Bowie's) class.[16]

As his brother John admitted, at times James had a bad temper. This was perhaps his worst trait. To compensate for it he repeatedly backed up his temper by risking his life. Mostly, however, he fought for principle and justice.

Capt. Archibald Hotchkiss of Palestine, Texas, first met Bowie in Washington City and saw him many times after that. He commented that Bowie had been in several violent transactions, but not on his own account, and remarked that he doubted if James ever fought a duel on his personal account.[17]

An incident relating to Bowie's honorableness in coming to the assistance of women, or to prevent a wrong, was related by

John J. Linn. In 1832 a couple came to San Felipe de Austin to get married, and put up at the boardinghouse of a Mrs. Payton. Under the Mexican law no one but a Catholic priest could perform a ceremony, but it was the custom then for marriages of convenience to be made. The prospective bride and groom would appear before the local *alcalde* and signify their intention to be wed, then live as man and wife until a priest would arrive in the town and a religious ceremony could be arranged.

The young bride-to-be was from the country, while the groom, from Arkansas, was supposedly a minister of the gospel. Bowie, who was also staying at the boardinghouse of Mrs. Payton, recognized the groom-to-be as a bogus preacher. The man was not only a horse thief in Arkansas but had fled that area, leaving behind a wife and several small children. James decided to prevent the marriage of convenience.

Bowie got a friend of his to impersonate a Catholic priest, and informed the *alcalde* of the background of the counterfeit minister. The *alcalde* readily agreed to Bowie's plan. When the happy couple arrived at the *alcalde*'s house to have the ceremony performed, they were told that a priest had arrived in town unexpectedly and would, under the law, have to perform a legitimate ceremony. As the priest spoke only Spanish, James Bowie would interpret for the couple. The bride happily agreed, and the phony minister also consented.

Shortly into the ceremony the counterfeit priest, as interpreted by Bowie, started inquiring of the groom about his past life in Arkansas, and related the many instances where he had stolen horses. Then, as the groom's brow started perspiring, Bowie started mentioning the names of the bogus minister's wife and children. When it became obvious that the man was trying to become a bigamist and had a living wife and children, Mrs. Payton put a stop to the proceedings and ordered the man from her house.[18]

CHAPTER 13

Bowie, The Fighting Machine

Bowie's fame as a fighter was legendary in the Southwest by the early 1830s. His brawl with Maj. Norris Wright on the streets of Alexandria and his participation in the sandbar fracas were widely publicized and gave the Bowie knife its first prominence. Contrary to Rezin's assertion that after the "chance medley" on the sandbar Bowie engaged in no other fights, Bowie is known to have participated in at least three other duels. Very likely, with his temperament, he engaged in several others.

So much of this very interesting man's life is shrouded in myth, rumor, and speculation that no one knows for certain how many fights James actually engaged in. According to stories concerning Bowie, he was involved in many "medleys," as Rezin described such encounters; however, there are so many very similar versions of fights concerning Bowie and various persons at different times and in different places that perhaps many were the same fight embellished by different people when relating the incident.

An authentic duel concerned a man named Sturdivant. John (Bloody) Sturdivant was a noted tough and thug who was well known in the underworld of Natchez-under-the-Hill, then the disreputable section of Natchez, Mississippi. He knew all the ways to make a crooked dollar, and one of them was by counterfeiting. An arsonist as well, Sturdivant was known to have burned to the ground the homes of four political opponents and to have killed at least three people.[1]

All of these were only side ways of gaining an unsavory reputation, as his primary way of making a dishonest living was by operating several of the worst gambling and vice dens in the area, dens that were well known to use crooked methods to fleece the unwary.

Sturdivant was exactly the sort of man that Bowie always detested on sight. In the following incident, Bowie would get his chance to stand up to the man.

Dr. William Lattimore was a wealthy planter with a large plantation in the country below Natchez. He annually raised a large crop of cotton, at that time the South's leading product. The doctor was well known and respected in his community, and had been a territorial delegate in Congress from Mississippi for 1803–1807 and 1813–1817. In 1837 he served as a delegate to the Constitutional Convention, and served as a commissioner to locate a state capital. In addition, he was a warm friend of James Bowie.

In 1829, Dr. Lattimore sent his son to the Natchez wharf to sell the year's cotton crop, with instructions to deposit the proceeds in a Natchez bank. Young Lattimore sold the crop at a good price and was on his way to a bank to deposit the funds he had received. Suddenly, he was accosted by a stranger who happened to be an employee of Sturdivant's, and whose job was to entice suckers to Bloody John's gambling dens.

The stranger turned on his professional charm to the inexperienced youth, and before long the two men were visiting several bars, where Sturdivant's man purchased all the drinks for his new friend. When young Lattimore was sufficiently lubricated, the stranger then took him to one of his boss' gambling halls. Within a short time, the culpable youth was relieved of the thousands of dollars he had received for the cotton crop. Then he was unceremoniously thrown out in the street with the warning to "keep your mouth shut and go home, or in the morning you'll be floating down the river."[2]

The disheveled and bewildered youth was discontentedly wandering back toward the cotton wharf — probably sadder and much wiser — wondering what sort of story he could tell his father. Then he happened to run into Bowie, whom he recognized. He promptly told James the story of his adventurous evening, and how he had lost all the money from his father's cotton crop. Bowie told him, "Come with me. We're going back to Sturdivant's and I'll get your money back for you."

When the two men arrived at the gambling hall, Bowie sat at

a faro game and started playing. It didn't take him long before he spotted the crooked dealer and his method of cheating. He got up from the table, stuck his knife into it, and said he would use it on the next man who cheated.

James was not a professional gambler by any means, but like so many men of the day he frequently gambled for pleasure and was adept at cards. Within a few hours he had won back all the money that Lattimore had lost. He turned his winnings over to his young friend and told him to go home and stay away from gambling halls in the future.

Bloody John was a notorious fighter and had long bragged that if he had been one of the participants in the sandbar affair, he would have seen to it that Bowie was dead instead of just cut up. Now that Bowie was in his dive, Sturdivant thought this was a good opportunity to make good his boast and at the same time to get revenge for the humiliation he had suffered at seeing Bowie catch his man at cheating and win thousands of dollars. He rashly proposed that Bowie fight him then and there.

"That's fine with me," replied Bowie. "How do you want to fight?"

Bloody John, who fancied himself as something of an expert with a knife, drew a knife from his belt and threw it upon the table. Bowie followed suit. The two men promptly removed their coats as the dealers pushed the tables aside, allowing the two antagonists room in which to fight.

Rules were then agreed upon. The two contestants were to have their left wrists bound together with a scarf, which Sturdivant provided. Each man was to wait until the count of three before the action could commence. Bowie then instructed young Lattimore, who was an interested spectator, to take a pistol from his, Bowie's, belt, and "use it quickly should anyone attempt to interfere."

One of the croupiers was selected as timekeeper. As he slowly counted, the two opponents stood with firm footing on the floor, watching each other warily. As soon as the count of three was reached, Bloody John made one quick stroke which Bowie parried. Bowie then, with a savage thrust of his own knife, slashed the tendons in Sturdivant's right arm. While the surprised gambler stood in pain and fury, with blood streaming down his injured arm, James stated that he could not kill a helpless man.

He then instructed one of the house men to untie his boss' wrists and take care of his wounds.[3]

The wounded hoodlum never forgot the injury he suffered at the hands of Bowie, and some months later he hired three assassins to ambush and kill his enemy.

When James was returning to Texas after purchasing his new Bowie knife from James Black, the three desperadoes were waiting for him in some underbrush. With their own knives in hand, they rushed at him. As one assailant seized the bridle of James' horse, the quick-thinking Bowie drew his own brand-new knife, reached over the horse's neck, and thrust it into the thug's neck and killed him. The second man succeeded in stabbing Bowie a glancing blow in the calf of his leg before James could dismount. Bounding from his saddle, Bowie made one swing upward with his new blade and disemboweled his second opponent. By this time the third hired thug had lost all heart in the affair and tried to run away, but Bowie overtook him and split his skull to the shoulders.[4]

Thus was the new Bowie knife, with the guard on the handle, baptized in blood, and its owner bestowed with even greater renown as a fighting man.

Bowie's kindness in righting wrongs and to those in trouble was well known, and is illustrated by the following story.

While once riding across a plantation on his way to Rapides, he saw a man cruelly beating his slave, whom he had tied to a tree. When the owner disregarded Bowie's demands that he stop whipping the slave, James dismounted his horse, went over to the slave, and with his knife cut the rope binding his hand and set him free. At this the owner flew into a rage, drew his pistol, and rushed upon James. When he pressed the trigger the gun misfired, and Bowie closed in on the man with his knife. The owner then tried to run away, but James was too quick for him. With a sweep of his knife Bowie slashed the man's pistol wrist, nearly severing the hand. While the now helpless slaveowner stood aghast, Bowie took off his neckerchief and constructed a tourniquet to stanch the flow of blood. He then took the man to the nearest doctor and paid all the medical bills.[5]

One of Bowie's alleged duels occurred one night in an unlit New Orleans room with an unnamed Creole dandy. While waiting for a signal from outside the room, the two barefooted men warily prowled the dark room, Bowie using his knife while his foe used a sword. When the opponents finally made contact, a quick thrust of Bowie's knife found its mark in the Creole and ended the fray.[6]

If all reports are true, John Sturdivant wasn't the only man Bowie fought with his wrists tied to his opponent. There is the reported fight he had with another man, left wrists tied, and with the two duelists standing within the confines of a small circle. If either man backed out of the circle, he was declared a coward.

There are two versions of another knife fight in which Bowie was supposed to have participated. The first version says Bowie's opponent was a Spaniard who owned a plantation near his on Bayou Terrebonne. It seems the Spaniard continually annoyed Bowie with insults until James finally had enough of the pettiness and challenged his annoyer to a duel. As the challenged, the Spaniard had the choice of weapons and chose knives, since he had a hunting knife with a long blade.

The two men were to fight stripped to the waist and astride a low bench, or some sort of trestle, which was embedded in the ground. When the signal for the fight to commence was given, Bowie quickly thrust his weapon into the Spaniard's abdomen while the latter was still drawing his long knife back to make his thrust.[7]

In another version of the same incident, the two antagonists were sitting on a log which spanned a stream. Their left wrists were tied, and since the men were both wearing buckskin breeches, the breeches were nailed to the log. When the action began, Bowie immediately killed his man with a quick thrust. His next move was to cut through the two men's breeches while his foe's corpse slipped off the log and was carried away by the stream.[8]

Bowie did not always resort to his knife in his duels. In at least one recorded incident he used a pistol, and as is so frequently mentioned in stories about him, he once more, in an act of chivalry, came to the aid of strangers in distress. In this case the story concerned a beautiful young bride and her foolish husband on a Mississippi riverboat.

From about 1830 and on for a number of years, the Mississippi River was infested with professional gamblers, many of them crooked, plying their trade on the steamers that slowly paddled up and down the mother of waters. The crooks had arrangements with many hotel clerks, bartenders, and others to let them know when wealthy people, or persons carrying large sums of money, were booked to travel on the boats. Then the gamblers would ingratiate themselves with the prospective victims during a leisurely ride down the river, and entice them into card games.

One version of the story concerning the newlyweds on a riverboat was written by a Maj. Ben C. Truman, who gave the year of the event as 1833. An anonymous account that was reprinted in the *Democratic Telegraph and Texas Register* on June 20, 1850, gave the date of the duel as 1835 and identified the crooked gambler Bowie fought, a detail that Major Truman, for some reason, omitted. In one account the boat on which the event occurred was the *Orleans,* and in another account it was the *Rob Roy.*

In the Truman version a young man from Natchez was returning from an extended trip to the North with his new bride. During his trip he had collected a huge sum of money. At Pittsburgh, the couple boarded another steamer headed for Louisville. On the trip to Louisville, the crooked gamblers talked their victim into playing cards and cleverly let him win large pots. Then, at Louisville, everyone changed steamers and boarded the *Orleans.* When the game was resumed the skilled gamblers started cheating, and it wasn't long before the gentleman from Natchez found himself broke.

At this point, enter our hero, James Bowie.

While the disconsolate bride poured out her story, Bowie patted her on the shoulder and assured her that he would take care of everything. He then went to the gamblers' table and, while watching their game, deliberately exposed a well-filled wallet. The gamblers took the bait and invited him to join them.

Bowie carefully watched the gamblers and bet very heavily until the pot on the table reached $100,000. Suddenly, Bowie caught the dealer slipping an extra card to one of the gamblers. He seized the recipient of the extra card by the wrist, drew out his knife, and told the crook to lay his cards on the table face down. He then threw his own hand, which consisted of four kings and a ten, on the table. Calmly, he told the crook to show his hand, and stated that if it consisted of six cards he would kill him. The gambler stood up from the table in a rage and demanded that the stranger should fight him at once. He also demanded to know his name. When Bowie quietly answered "James Bowie," the other two gamblers shut up. They had heard of him and knew his reputation. The other man, who had never heard the name Bowie before, insisted on a duel with pistols at once. The place for the duel was to be the hurricane deck of the *Orleans*.

At the hurricane deck roof the two principals climbed upon the top of each wheelhouse, which were about twelve yards apart. The rules agreed upon were that the second would utter the words "one, two, three, fire, stop" at intervals of one second each. As "one" rang out, each man raised his pistol; as "three" was uttered the gambler fired and missed; and just as "fire" was spoken, Bowie fired and struck the gambler. The gambler fell to the deck of the steamer, and then rolled off into the river. Bowie then took the $100,000 to the newlyweds and divided the money, giving them two-thirds while keeping one-third for himself.[9]

The version printed in the *Democratic Telegraph and Texas Register* was virtually the same in all essentials, but had minor variations. It gave the name of the steamer as being the *Rob Roy*, and placed the date of the affair as being the evening of June 4, 1835. The amount at stake was only $20,000, and the gambler who was shot and killed by Bowie was none other than John Lafitte, illegitimate son of the pirate Jean Lafitte.

In this version, Lafitte's bullet snipped off one of Bowie's "golden locks," and Lafitte was shot through the heart. His body, as in the first version, rolled off the deck into the waters of the Mississippi. Bowie, as gallantly as ever, returned the young couple's money to them, and was rewarded by them with many gracious thanks.[10]

Ranger Capt. Andrew J. Sowell, in an article he wrote for the *San Antonio Light* on May 4, 1917, stated that the incident in which Lafitte was killed on a Mississippi riverboat happened in 1830.[11] With all the varied evidence at hand, it does seem as though this is at least one authentic gun duel in which Bowie engaged during his lifetime.

The Jacksboro (Texas) *Echo* of May 25, 1877, reported an incident in which Bowie apparently fought at least one formal duel with a Spaniard, and rifles were the weapons used.

The participants were to stand back to back and hold the

rifles perpendicular, upward or downward as they desired. At the command of "wheel," each party was supposed to wheel and commence firing. While the Spaniard was executing the usual military maneuver of turning, Bowie simply turned his body on his hip while his feet were still braced on the ground, and fired his bullet through his foe's brain.[12]

Bowie is also said to have had a fist fight with his actor friend, Edwin Forrest, in a gambling house. The two men were competing for a girl. Although the place, date, and outcome are unspecified, with his lean, husky physique and his known fighting qualities as always being a winner, it is a pretty good bet that James won the fight.

Truly, if Bowie had engaged in only one-half of the encounters he was reputed to have been in—and won—he most certainly was a one-man engine of destruction.

CHAPTER 14

The Restless Man

Despite James' great love for Ursula, his fondness for the Veramendis, and his contentment in Bexar, his restless nature would take over and he would frequently be away from home.

Rezin was having trouble with his eyes, so in 1832 Bowie accompanied him to Philadelphia so that Rezin could consult with a prominent physician, Dr. William Pepper.[1] John S. Moore, a grandson of Rezin, wrote to Col. Wm. Winton Fontaine of Austin and related how Rezin had been stricken with blindness and had gone to Philadelphia to see Dr. Joseph Parrish. Rezin had also gone to see Dr. Valentine Mott of New York, a celebrated surgeon of 25 Park Place, to receive treatment with the result that one eye partially recovered its sight. It could have been on one of these occasions that Rezin wrote his version of the celebrated encounter with the Indians at the San Saba mines for a Philadelphia newspaper. Henderson Yoakum, a prominent Texan of that time, and later on Sam Houston's lawyer, described that encounter as a "model Indian fight."[2]

During January of 1832, Bowie was granted permission in San Antonio to raise an expedition against the Tawakonis, since he estimated they had 2,000 horses worth capturing. A rumor promptly spread that the object of the expedition was to "further the views of speculators in mines," and a hot advertisement against the rumor was published.[3] This expedition might very well have been the one that Bowie led through Indian territory without spotting an Indian.

For some years there had been rumblings of discontent against the Mexican government, and matters started worsening in 1830. On January 1 of that year, Gen. Anastasio Bustamante had taken office as president of Mexico, and on April 6 a decree known as "Bustamante's law" went into effect. This law became the turning point in the relations of the Texas colonists and the Mexican government, since it incorporated many features the Anglo settlers heartily disliked.

The law prohibited further American immigration into the colony while encouraging the immigration of Europeans, particularly from Switzerland and Germany.[4] In addition, the law proposed to settle Mexican convicts in Coahuila–Texas after their release from prison and military service, and peons were encouraged to settle there in return for land that would be given them.

New customs duties that restricted trade with other nations were imposed, and all land grants were suspended unless at least 100 colonists had already settled in the areas allotted. In addition, the government promptly established military posts at Nacogdoches, Anahuac, Velasco, San Antonio de Bexar, Goliad, and other points.

Friction continued to increase between the Mexican authorities and the Texas Anglos. During the summer of 1832, angry Texans engaged Mexican troops in military actions at Anahuac, at the mouth of the Trinity River near Galveston Bay, and at Velasco, at the mouth of the Brazos. Bowie had not participated in either of those actions, but when, on August 2, a group of disgruntled Texans marched into Nacogdoches to present their demands to Col. Jose de las Piedras, commander of the post, Bowie was among them.

Just north of the Stone House, a building housing the *alcalde* and other officials of the town, the small force was suddenly attacked by a force of around 100 Mexican cavalry. The Battle of Nacogdoches had begun. The charge was beaten off, but in the exchange of rifle fire the Mexicans shot and killed Don Encarnasion Chireno, the *alcalde*.[5] The Texans took possession of the houses on the north and south sides of the square, and their accurate marksmanship took a toll on every Mexican showing himself. During the evening, the Mexicans made one sortie that was repulsed. Later that night, Piedras and his troops fled, leaving behind his killed and wounded.

Bowie was promptly dispatched with twenty men to pursue Piedras and his troops and caught up with them some twenty miles from San Antonio. After some gunfire, Piedras surrendered. He was then sent back to Mexico, and Bowie and his men escorted 310 officers and men to San Felipe de Austin.[6]

During December of that year, Bowie was in Austin on business when he ran into an old friend he had met a few years previously in Helena. Sam Houston had recently crossed the Red River after a three-year exile among the Cherokees in what is now Oklahoma. He planned to settle in Nacogdoches and make Texas his permanent home, and was in town to see Stephen F. Austin and secure a grant of land as a single man. Austin, however, was not at home, being engaged in business elsewhere in his vast domain.

Houston and Bowie quickly renewed their friendship and decided to have Christmas dinner in the city. They then rode together to San Antonio, where Bowie introduced the former governor of Tennessee to Ursula and the Veramendi family, and to Francisco Antonio Ruiz, the town's *alcalde*.

A number of prominent Texans were crying for independence from Mexico, and conventions were being held to discuss Texas being severed from Coahuila and granted status as an independent state. Bowie was among those present as a delegate to the Colonial Convention of 1833, the one which drew up the second memorial requesting independent statehood.

In contrast to many prominent Texans who were exhibiting dissatisfaction with the Mexican government, Bowie had little to gain and much to lose in any conflict between the Anglos and the Mexicans. His social and business interests were focused in Mexican communities such as Bexar in Texas and Saltillo and Monclova in Coahuila, where he had his wool mills. As an Anglo and as a very active land speculator, he was highly dependent upon the good will of Mexican officials; in addition, the special taxes and other punitive measures levied against other North Americans did not affect him. Monclova and Saltillo, where he maintained homes, were not subjected to garrison rule, as were so many cities in the Texas portion of the dual state. Finally, as a highly regarded in-law to the influential Veramendi family, he was certainly a privileged character.

Suddenly, Bowie's life of happiness was shattered. In 1833, Mexico and certain portions of Texas were struck by a violent cholera epidemic and it was feared that the plague might extend as far as San Antonio.

Bowie was planning an extended business trip east to Louisiana and Mississippi, and he did not want his family in San Antonio if the epidemic struck there. Since he believed the mountainous country of Coahuila would be much safer, he sent his wife and their one child to his estate in Monclova, promising to join her there in September or October. Since Ursula was pregnant, the entire Veramendi family accompanied her, including the Veramendis' adopted son and some family retainers.

The epidemic finally struck Monclova with harsh severity. In the period of September 5–18, 571 persons lost their lives to the disease.[7] Between the sixth and fourteenth of the month, Ursula and her two children (she had given birth to a son) and the entire Veramendi family were wiped out. In Texas, the virulent cholera also claimed the life of the brother of Stephen F. Austin. Austin caught the disease and for days was near death, but finally recovered.

In Natchez on October 21, 1833, and unaware yet of the death of his wife and their children, Bowie executed and signed his will. Perhaps he did this because of the death of his brother Stephen a few months previously. In the instrument he designated as his sole heirs his brother Rezin, their sister Martha Bowie Sterrett, and her husband, Alexander B. Sterrett. Out of his estate he specified that $4,000 be paid to Dr. Samuel Gustine, who had advanced him that amount. He left another $4,000 to Dr. Addison Dashiel, as the doctor had stood as security for him.

"To my dearly beloved wife, M. Bowie . . . I leave the jewelry which I purchased for her." Other than the jewelry he left Ursula nothing, explaining that he had previously provided for her.[8] He also stipulated that his nephew and niece, James A. and Marian Bowie, children of his recently deceased brother Stephen, be educated out of the proceeds of his estate.

Bowie was lying ill at the home of his friend Angus McNeill in Mississippi when word of the death of his family and the Veramendis reached him. He was completely devastated at the news and from then on was a completely changed man. He began drinking more heavily and was careless in his dress.[9] When he recovered from his illness he left Mississippi for Louisiana to mourn his loss in the bosom of his family.

Eventually he returned to Texas, and from there proceeded to Saltillo and Monclova to dispose of his manufacturing interests there at a great sacrifice.

The year 1834 was an active one for Bowie, and he was constantly on the move between Texas, Louisiana, Mississippi, and Mexico. Some of this might have been done in an effort to overcome his grief at the loss of his beloved Ursula and the two children — one whom he scarcely knew and the other he had never seen. Some of his traveling was probably due to his natural wanderlust, and some of it was due to his becoming more active in political affairs.

On a visit to New Orleans, James had his portrait painted by Benjamin West, the celebrated artist, before returning to San Antonio. He then went to Coahuila and became an agent for John T. Mason in 400-league land deals, and was still there during the early months of 1835.[10]

On March 29, 1833, Gen. Antonio López de Santa Anna had been elected president of Mexico without opposition and set in motion his centralist policies of government. He promptly assumed dictatorial powers, and as he hated *norteamericanos* he promptly showed his hostility toward Anglos in Texas.

In 1833 the legislature had passed an act providing for the removal of the capital of Coahuila–Texas from Saltillo in the south to Monclova in the north. This caused a tremendous quarrel between the two sections, but in 1834, when Santa Anna decided the issue in favor of Monclova, the representatives of Saltillo withdrew from the legislature and set up a separate government. In the resulting confusion it became impossible to hold the regular election of state officials.[11]

As relations between Texas and Mexico worsened, Mexicans increasingly looked upon the public lands of Texas as virtually valueless. The Coahuila legislature in 1834 and 1835 granted away millions of acres of Texas lands for a trifle, and this antagonized many responsible Texans. John T. Mason, representing both himself and a New York syndicate, in 1834 had acquired titles to 300 leagues and in 1835 to 1,100 leagues, which represented more than 6,250,000 acres.

In early 1835 James Bowie was made special land commissioner by the Coahuila and Texas government to issue titles on the Mason grants. In September, he signed away titles to eleven league tracts of land that aggregated close to half a million acres.[12] Later on, one of the first acts of the provisional government of Texas would be to nullify titles to the Mason and other grants of land acquired under "suspicious circumstances." The Texas Constitution that was adopted on March 17, 1836, declared "each and every grant made to John T. Mason null and void from the beginning."[13]

Shortly after Bowie became a land agent for Mason, he promptly became involved in the dispute between Saltillo and Monclova.

The act of the legislature caused Santa Anna to send in his brother-in-law, Gen. Martín Perfecto de Cos, to occupy Monclova. Subsequently, several Texans who were in Monclova on business, including Ben Milam and John Cameron, were arrested and jailed. James Bowie and José Maria Carbajal were among those escaping arrest. They promptly returned to Texas to report that the government and legislative deputies were in prison, and that all vessels in the port at Matamoros were embargoed to await the arrival of 3,000 troops from Saltillo to be transported to Texas.[14]

Spencer S. Jack, one of the Texans in Coahuila during those days, later wrote a report of his trip, in which he stated:

> At the time we were in Coahuila [1834] there was exhibited the singular spectacle of two governors and two Congresses in session, in the same State and not more than 100 miles distant from each other. In the contest, Colonel Bowie took an active and decided part in favor of the government in Monclova and at one time when the armies of the two towns lay within a few miles of each other nearby on the halfway ground, Bowie did everything in his power to bring on a battle.[15]

Bowie was still in Monclova during the early months of 1835, but by July he had returned to Texas and Louisiana. John Forbes wrote to his friend James B. Miller on July 24, 1835, and said, "Colonel Bowie is ever alive to the interests of Texas." He continued with an account of how Bowie, on certain occasions, had boldly intercepted dispatches from the Mexican government to its consul in New Orleans.[16]

Matters were rapidly worsening between the Texans and the Mexican government. When Santa Anna had approved the moving of the capital of Coahuila–Texas from Saltillo to Monclova, he had virtually abolished the military. This act infuriated the colonists because they were surrounded by hostile Indians, who outnumbered them greatly.[17]

When the dictator also abolished the state legislatures, most of those south of the Rio Grande acquiesced, but the province of Zacatecas resisted and refused to surrender their weapons. For their impudence Santa Anna placed himself at the head of his army and marched upon the province. After a bloody battle on May 11, 1835, his troops overwhelmed the luckless Zacatecans, killing some 2,000 of them and taking 2,700 prisoners. Not satisfied, the victors marched into the capital and for the next two days engaged in the butchery of the unfortunate inhabitants and plundered their city. When news of this atrocity reached the Anglo-Americans, they were horrified, and talks of complete independence from Mexico were being heard in many quarters.

The Anglos were further dismayed when captured documents from General Cos to Capt. Antonio Tenorio, the commandant of Anahuac, revealed that Santa Anna was sending into Texas a strong division of the troops which had butchered Zacatecas. The documents showed that it was clearly his intention to give the Texans a dose of the same harsh medicine he had given the Zacatecans, and to expel all Anglo-Americans who had arrived in the colony since 1830.

The fires were inflated a little more in early June, when a respected merchant named Andrew Briscoe had been placed in the Anahuac jail for a practical joke. The impetuous young lawyer William Barret Travis promptly led a volunteer force of twenty-five men to Anahuac, in the Texas portion of the dual state at the mouth of the Trinity River near Galveston Bay. After a brief fracas, Travis and his men liberated Briscoe, Tenorio surrendered, and he and his men were provided with arms to defend themselves against Indians. They were then sent back to Mexico after the captain gave his pledge that neither he nor his troops would fight in Texas again.

In August, Bowie visited friendly Shawnee and Cherokee villages, ostensibly on an inspection assignment for Henry Ruez, the political boss of Nacogdoches. However, his primary purpose was to determine the pulse of the Indians and the extent of their loyalty to Mexico in the forthcoming struggle so many foresaw.[18]

In late September, Col. Domingo de Ugartechea, the commandant of Texas who was headquartered at San Antonio de Bexar, had sent a force under the command of Lt. Francisco Castaneda to Gonzales, a small town seventy miles east of San Antonio. Some four years previously, the colonists at Gonzales had been furnished a six-pound brass cannon for their defense against the Indians. As part of a general plan to disarm the Texans, Castaneda was under instructions to take back this cannon.

When the Texans rejected Castaneda's demand to surrender the cannon, the lieutenant positioned his forces on a small hill by the Guadalupe River and waited, but by October 1 he had made no attempt to attack. The Texans, then about 150 strong, elected John H. Moore as their colonel, and that night under cover of darkness they crossed the river and took up a position opposite the Mexicans. Filling their cannon with scrap iron, they painted "Come and Take It" on the weapon in large letters and placed it in full view of the enemy.

Since Castaneda did not respond to the challenge, Colonel Moore sent a messenger at dawn, asking him to surrender. When the Mexican lieutenant refused, Moore ordered his Texans to fire the cannon and to advance. The Mexicans promptly panicked and retreated toward San Antonio to join their main body. The Texans, who had suffered no losses, collected whatever booty their foe had left behind.

It was October 5, 1835, and the Texas War for Independence was now officially on.

CHAPTER 15

War Begins

The drama of Texas' fight for independence from Mexico had been gathering steam since around 1832. Beginning in that year, any personalities who were to have prominent parts in the coming revolution had arrived.

Sam Houston, former governor of Tennessee, after a three-year self-imposed exile among the Cherokees in the Cherokee Nation West, had moved to Texas and settled in Nacogdoches to practice law. James Bonham and the twenty-seven-year-old, red-haired William Barret Travis, childhood friends from South Carolina, were lawyers, and bachelor Ben Milam had been speculating in land in Texas. James Fannin, former West Point dropout and slave runner, had also arrived. And, of course, Stephen Fuller Austin and James Bowie were ever present.

It was Austin's father, Moses Austin of Durham, Connecticut, who had first come up with the idea of settling an Anglo colony in the province of Texas. He had made application to the authorities in Mexico to bring in settlers, and on January 17, 1821, had received a grant of 200,000 acres and was given permission to bring in 300 families. Due to the slowness of communication in those days, news of the grant did not reach him until the following June. He died of pneumonia a few days later, but persuaded his son Stephen to carry on his dream.[1]

As an empresario, Stephen was given considerable leeway in ruling his colony and was authorized to organize and command militia. On October 6, 1835, the Committee of Safety for the municipality of Nacogdoches, meeting in San Augustine, appointed Sam Houston as general and commander-in-chief of the forces of the Nacogdoches Department, and granted him full power to raise troops, organize the forces, and do all other things pertaining to that office.[2]

When news circulated that General Cos was at the head of 400 men marching on their way to San Antonio to confiscate the property of the rebellious citizens, mass meetings were held and offers were made to buy rifles for the first fifty recruits.

After the skirmish at Gonzales, volunteers to the army flocked there, and on the evening of October 10 they elected Stephen Austin their commander-in-chief. Their intention was to set off within two days to attack San Antonio with a force of 500 men and the six-pounder they had retained. Austin accepted the command and departed from Goliad with Fannin, Travis, Milam, Bonham, and others, to join his troops. By late October he and his men were in a camp at Salado Creek, about five miles east of San Antonio. He made use of his scouts and spies to keep himself informed of the activities of the enemy troops. Instead of going on the attack, he sent General Cos a note to see if a compromise could not be worked out. Cos replied: "I shall never treat with the ungrateful Texans save as rebels."[3]

Among the volunteers who joined Austin was James Bowie, who had come galloping into camp on a small gray mare with six volunteers from Louisiana, his famous knife secured in his sash and a rifle slung from his saddle.[4]

On October 22 Austin wrote a letter addressed to Col. James Bowie, directing him and Capt. James W. Fannin to reconnoiter the missions of San Francisco de la Espada and San Jose y San Miguel de Aguayo to procure supplies for the army. Juan N. Seguin was a captain in Austin's volunteer army and a wealthy citizen of San Antonio. He had a ranch south of the town, and had given the Texans permission to use his property as a source for whatever provisions they needed.

On the morning of October 24, Bowie sent a courier to Austin requesting reinforcements of fifty men. Later that morning he sent a letter to Austin, addressing him as General Austin, and asked for an additional 150 since he and Fannin had the road to Rio Grande and various missions to guard, and he was expecting an attack that night by some enemy troops. Signing the letter "Colonel" Bowie, he also suggested to Austin that if he, Bowie, was superseded by any officer, that General Houston should succeed him. Austin sent the reinforcements.

Although in some correspondence Austin would refer to Bowie as "Colonel" Bowie, James never received a commission. This rankled him, particularly since Fannin had been given a captaincy. He was unhappier still when, on October 24, Austin acknowledged his reports of the 22 and 23 and addressed them as "James Bowie, Esq., and Captain Fannin."[5]

On October 27 Bowie received the following order from Austin from his headquarters at Mission Espada. It was addressed to "Col. James Bowie, Volunteer Aide":

> You will proceed with the first division of Captain Fannin's company and others attached to that division and select the best and most secure position that can be had on the river, as near Bejar as practicable to encamp the army tonight, keeping in view in the selection of this position pasturage and the security of the horses, and the army from night attacks of the enemy.
>
> You will also reconnoiter, so far as time and circumstances will permit, the situation of the outskirts of the town and the approaches to it, whether the houses have been destroyed on the outside, so as to leave every approach exposed to the raking of the cannon.
>
> You will make your report with *as little delay as possible,* SO AS TO GIVE TIME TO THE ARMY TO MARCH AND TAKE UP ITS POSITION BEFORE NIGHT. Should you be attacked by a large force, send expresses *immediately* with the particulars.[6]

Bowie and Fannin took ninety-two men with them. Many of their contingent were members of the New Orleans Grays who had recently joined the Texas forces, and a number of these were boys aged fourteen to twenty-two.

The two commanders hurried to accomplish their task, and finally selected a position within a mile and a half of San Antonio, in the bend of the San Antonio River and some 500 yards from the old mission of Nuestra Senora de la Purisima Concepción de Acuna, commonly referred to as the mission Concepción.

Rather than take their weary troops and horses back to join Austin and his men, the two commanders picked a good defensive position and decided to camp there for the night. They sent a message to Austin by David M. Macomb that the place had been chosen too late to return to the main army.

A level plain in the bend of the river was bordered by heavily wooded land, to form two nearly equal sides of a broad wedge. A steep decline dropped some six to ten feet to the river bottom so that the river itself protected the rear, and the area provided a natural fortification against any artillery fire. The strategy was for the men to dig steps in the bluff, and if an attack came, half of the men would go up the steps and fire, then drop back to reload while the other half replaced them and continued the firing.

With Fannin's Brazos Guards on one side of the bend, and Bowie's *Los Leoncitos* on the other, it was virtually impossible for an attacking force to form an effective frontal charge, and it was difficult for any cavalry to encircle the defenders because of the river. Sentries were then posted for the night.

On the morning of October 28, Cos approached in the fog with his force of about 300 infantry, 100 cavalry, and two small cannons. The fog began lifting at around 8:00 and the Mexican infantry advanced to about 200 yards on the Texans' right and opened fire; however, it was ineffective due to the excellent defensive position of the Texans. When the firing began, Noah Smithwick, who was near Bowie, remembered him cautioning: "Keep under cover, boys . . . we haven't a man to spare."

After about ten minutes, Cos moved one of his six-pounders up to fire at a range of eighty yards, but it, too, proved ineffective. When the Mexican cannoneers would stop to reload, the Texans would move up the bluff and pick them off. Finally, after several ineffective charges by the infantry and cavalry, and his artillery having absolutely no effect, Cos retreated with his demoralized troops. The Texans had won the Battle of Concepción, with a loss of one man killed and none wounded. The Mexicans had lost nearly ten men killed and wounded, including some officers.

In his later report to Austin, Bowie mentioned that after about ten minutes of the action, the Mexicans started firing a brass double-fortified four-pounder, using grape and canisters, about eighty yards from the right flank of the first division, and a charge was sounded. However, he reported, "the cannon was cleared, as if by magic, and a check put to the charge." What he failed to mention, although others did, was that he personally led the charge to seize the cannon and that it was the turning point in the battle.[7]

Inasmuch as Bowie and Fannin had commanded for what

was briefly an independent division, it is possible that it was after this fight that the report spread eastward that Bowie was, in fact, at the head of the army. Houston wrote to congratulate both him and the army.[8]

About an hour after the skirmish was over, Austin and the main army arrived and made camp. Operations at Bexar then ground to a halt.

When Bowie and Fannin submitted to Austin their official report of their joint operation, Bowie signed the report first as "James Bowie, Aid-de-camp." Fannin placed his signature under that of Bowie's, signing himself as "Commandant, first division."

Cos made no further attempt to go on the attack, so on October 31 Bowie penciled a letter to him:

> You are aware of the position of the forces under my command below Bexar, as well as that of General Austin's above town. The two bodies are now prepared to act in concert with each other, but before further hostilities are resumed, I am induced by the most friendly and humane considerations for my Mexican fellow citizens to open a communication with you in order to close the war and unnecessary effusion of blood. I fought you on the 28th with only a small detachment of ninety-two men.
>
> Should you feel disposed to enter into negotiations for the accomplishment of this desirable object, your flag will be respected. In this event war may be speedily and honorably closed and the rights of all secured. Your answer will be expected this afternoon
>
> With sentiments of the highest consideration for your excellency's happiness, I am yours, etc.
>
> James Bowie
>
> And trust that you will allow the volunteers who are just from their homes, accustomed to agricultural pursuits only, fought you like men resolved to live free or die. They have sworn to support and maintain the federal constitution of 1824, and they hold to that as their sheet anchor and will sooner part with life than abandon it without further effort. It is with much difficulty those brave men can be now restrained having been reinforced by a large number of their countrymen and recently flushed with victory purchased at no loss on their part.[9]

On November 2, at a council of war, Austin asked his officers for their opinion as to the advisability of a direct assault upon the heavily fortified Mexican position in the Alamo, since the Texans had no heavy artillery to support any attack. Besides, scouts reported that Cos' army had now been increased to 1,100 men.

When Austin called for a vote to attack or not, Bowie, Fannin, Milam, Edward Burleson, and all other officers present, with one exception, voted against an attack. The prevailing opinion, in which Austin concurred, was that it would be wiser to lay a siege and wait for more cannon and additional reinforcements. Accordingly, on November 2 the Texans began their siege of Cos and his men.

Bowie was a man of action, and as a fighting man he was becoming more and more disenchanted with the minor tasks of scouting and spying that he had been given. To him, the title of "volunteer aid" meant absolutely nothing. He and Austin had never been the closest of friends, and rightly or wrongly he suspected that the latter was withholding a commission because he so strongly disapproved of the actions of Bowie and others in their various land speculations.

Two days after the Battle of Concepción, Bowie tendered his resignation to Austin, stating in his letter: "I have declined further action under the appointment given to me by yourself. This, you will, therefore, look upon as my resignation. I will be found in Captain Fannin's company, where my duty to my country and the principles of human rights shall be discharged on my part, to the extent of my abilities as a private." [10]

Perhaps in order to assuage Bowie, on November 4 Austin offered him a temporary position as adjutant general. Bowie accepted the post, but then two days later once more resigned. [11]

The besieged General Cos, on the morning of November 26, had sent out a party of over 100 men on the old Presidio Road to cut grass for his horses. They were on their way back and were about five miles from San Antonio when they were spotted by Deaf Smith, one of the Texan scouts. Smith immediately reported to his superiors what he had seen, and everyone was of the opinion that it was Col. Domingo de Ugartechea bringing reinforcements and the payroll to Cos.

Bowie, with about a hundred mounted men, immediately set out to intercept the party and met the enemy about a mile from town. The Mexicans promptly took up their position in the bed of a dry gulch.

Cos had seen the Texans leave the town and sent out a detachment with two pieces of artillery to defend the foraging party. Just as Bowie charged the right of the foragers, Cos' troops came up on the left, and a brief battle ensued. The main body of Austin's troops, which had been behind Bowie and his men, now arrived and entered the fray. The fighting became a general melee; the Mexicans started retreating and a running fight began with Bowie and his mounted cavalry chasing them.

When the Grass Fight, as it became known, was over, the Texans had two wounded, one missing, and none killed. In addition, they had captured seventy horses.[12]

CHAPTER 16

Cast of Characters

On November 3, 1835, with a quorum present, fifty-five members representing the thirteen municipalities of Texas met in San Felipe de Austin in a narrow, one-room building. Their purpose was to form a provisional government of Texas.

The government the delegates came up with provided for a governor and a general council with weakly defined and almost coordinate powers. Henry Smith from Brazoria was elected governor by nine votes over Stephen F. Austin; James W. Robinson was elected lieutenant governor.

In a letter to the consultation, Austin requested that he be relieved from command of the army. His request was granted. In his place, Sam Houston was elected major general and commander-in-chief of all the forces called into public service during the war. He was authorized to recruit both regulars and volunteers for his army, but was given authority to appoint officers only to his personal staff; the council retained authority to grant all other commissions. Austin then ordered his men in San Antonio to elect a temporary commander to succeed him. They did, and elected Col. Edward Burleson. Although Burleson was a good friend of his, Bowie was hurt that he had not been chosen for the post.

Bowie was still trying to get a commission in the army but never achieved his goal. He even appeared before the general council and with hat in hand addressed that body for an hour, pleading for a commission.[1] The council turned him down, but on December 7 granted Fannin a commission as colonel of artillery in the regular army. William Barret Travis was offered a commission as major of artillery in the regular army, turned it down, and then accepted a commission as lieutenant colonel of cavalry. Houston, a staunch friend of Bowie, offered James a commission as an officer on his staff. Bowie turned it down inasmuch as he wanted to command a regiment in the line.

Houston tried his best to get the council to offer Bowie a commission, but had to confess failure. He always had a high regard for James, and told friends that Bowie was a born leader and a soldier of marked ability. Houston complained that his inability to secure a commission for Bowie was because of the dislike of Wyatt Hanks, chairman of the Military Affairs Committee, for himself. Another reason was that members of the council and their political backers had never forgiven Bowie for his land speculations, as authorized by the Monclova legislature.

The siege of San Antonio was still in force. Cos, awaiting reinforcements, was wary of attacking the Texans. There were minor skirmishes between scouts and outposts of the two armies, but no serious engagements.

The Texans were getting restless, and with the inactivity their troops had dwindled to around 400 men. With the siege at a stalemate and the season for the cold, biting "northers" at hand, there was discussion as to whether to continue the siege or to retire to Goliad. Their strength was about half that of Cos, they knew he had requested reinforcements from Mexico, and there were rumors that Santa Anna himself would soon be marching into Texas with an army of 10,000.

Goliad was the perfect place for the army to move to if they lifted the siege. There, Texas troops could cut off the enemy's communication with the seaboard, keep the frontier under observation, and it was an excellent point from which to march in the event of any hostile movements being made by Santa Anna's troops upon Texas frontier settlements.

On November 24, 1835, and just about the time he gave up command of his army, Austin sent out an order from his headquarters. Headed "Headquarters of the Federal Army of Texas," he ordered Bowie to Goliad to investigate the situation there.[2]

On December 3 the army at San Antonio had about decided to move to winter quarters at Goliad when the situation suddenly changed. The next day, Lt. Jesus "Comanche" Cuellar, a Mexican officer who had deserted from Cos' army, came into camp. He brought information that the strength of the Mexican forces had been overestimated, that their camp was highly disorganized, and that their morale was poor.[3]

The Texans quizzed Cuellar thoroughly and decided he was telling the truth, and concluded that an attack upon the town and the Alamo was feasible. The grizzled veteran Ben Milam, who had escaped from the Monclova prison, stepped in front of head-quarters and cried, "Who will follow old Ben Milam into San Antonio?" Three hundred volunteers stepped forward. Burleson gave his assent for the attack, but stayed in camp with the reserve forces.

The volunteer unit was separated into two commands, one being given to Milam and the other to Francis W. Johnson. The plan was for the attack to begin at twenty minutes before daylight on December 5, with the first two columns to attack the town proper, while a side maneuver under the command of Lt. Col. James C. Neill was to make a feint on the Alamo to divert attention.

The assault began at the appointed hour and the battle became a grueling one, with the Texans literally going from house to house, tunneling themselves inside with the use of crowbars to cut holes through the roofs or walls. On the third day, the gallant Milam was killed when he was struck in the head by a sniper's bullet as he entered the courtyard of former vice-governor Veramendi, Bowie's late father-in-law, near the Plaza. Milam fell in Sam Maverick's arms.[4]

On December 9 Cos asked for terms of capitulation while the battle still raged. The articles of surrender were signed on the eleventh and Cos, giving his parole to leave Texas and not return, departed for Mexico and took his beaten army with him. During the battle the Texans had twelve killed and eighteen wounded. It was estimated the Mexicans suffered 150 killed and an untold number wounded. When Capt. José Juan Sanchez Navarro was appointed by Cos to sign the surrender document, he moaned: "All has been lost save honor."[5]

On December 15 Cos wrote Santa Anna a whining letter, giving many alibis as to how he, with a superior force, had been defeated by the Texans.[6] On the same day, Burleson resigned his command and went home to his family. Col. Francis W. Johnson, who had played an active part in the storming of San Antonio, was elected to take his place.

Where was Bowie when the Battle of San Antonio was taking place? There are conflicting reports, as some say he and Travis were on a scouting mission around the Rio Grande. Others say he took part in the battle, and was a witness to the signing of the document of surrender. This is just another of the many conflicting stories that surround this remarkable man.

After Cos and his defeated troops left Bexar heading toward Mexico, the Texas army rapidly became highly disorganized, restless, and unruly. Everyone thought the war was over. Even before the Battle of Concepción, the men had been undisciplined, and now that the Mexican army had left for Mexico they became more so.

Virtually all of the Texas troops were volunteers and could come and go as they desired. The 188 who would later defend the Alamo came from seven different nations and twenty-two states, including Texas. Of the Texans, only nine were born in Texas, and eight of them were Mexicans. Many were frontiersmen, and many came from disparate occupations.

There was red-headed, tobacco-chewing Henry Warnell, a 118-pound jockey from Arkansas; Almeron Dickinson, a blacksmith from Tennessee; Micajah Autry, a poet from North Carolina; and John, a young black slave who had been deserted by his master. There were farmers, and some medical doctors. George Kemble from New York was a hatter. From England came Stephen Dennison, a painter. Young Christopher Parker's grandfather had been with Washington at Valley Forge, and there was James N. Rose, whose uncle was former president James Madison. Two-thirds had been in Texas less than six years.

Many were very young, ranging in age from fourteen to twenty, and had come to Texas from various southern states on a lark, wanting to throw their lot in with the colonists. Few of the men were used to taking orders from anyone, and a number of them left the army to go home to their families and farms. Those who stayed behind had very low morale as they had received no pay for their efforts, and food, provisions, and clothing were scarce.

Lieutenant Colonel Neill wrote the general council to com-
plain about the lack of food and clothing, and stated that many of
the volunteers were down to one shirt and one blanket, adding
that "if there has ever been a dollar here, I have no knowledge of
it." Conditions worsened, so Neill moved his men from the town
of Bexar back across the winding little San Antonio River into the
old mission, just east of town, known as the Alamo.

Into this demoralized situation stepped Dr. James Grant, a
Scot who had served valiantly during the Battle of San Antonio.
Grant had never lived in the Texas portion of the dual state, but
had resided in Coahuila. There, he had had vast estates and had
been a member of the legislature until he had a falling out with
Santa Anna. As a result, the dictator had confiscated the estates
and Grant had promptly moved to Texas and joined the Texan
cause. Naturally, he wanted his estates back.

Grant proposed to his fellow soldiers that they undertake an
expedition to Matamoros, located about 275 miles slightly
southwest from San Antonio, and across the Rio Grande, and
then into the interior of Mexico, where he could liberate his
estates at Parras.

When Grant painted a rosy picture of the rich spoils to be
taken from the cities of Tamaulipas, Nuevo Leon, Coahuila, and
San Luis Potosi, his proposals fell on willing ears among the rest-
less volunteers and adventurers who were still in the army in San
Antonio. But when word of the scheme reached the office of
Governor Smith, he violently opposed the plan. So did Gen. Sam
Houston, who considered it militarily unsound and little short of
piracy.

Despite the opposition of Smith and Houston, the council,
still at odds with the governor, authorized the venture and offered
the command of the expedition to Frank Johnson. Johnson
declined.

While Austin was still in command of the army, and after the
Battle of Concepción, Fannin had resigned for "personal reasons." He had then asked Houston to make him a brigadier
general but Houston refused, instead offering him the post of
inspector general with the rank of colonel. Fannin had refused
the appointment but had managed to secure from the council a
commission as colonel in the regular army.

The council, which was constantly meddling in military

affairs, had come up with the ambiguous rank of "military agent." The holder of this position would serve as field commander and would be responsible not to Houston, as commander-in-chief, but to the council.

When Johnson declined to lead the troops to Matamoros, the council then offered the post to Fannin. He promptly accepted, and then Johnson changed his mind and wanted to lead the venture. In their indecisiveness, the council authorized him to do so and did not bother to notify Fannin. Grant then got into the act by claiming the proposed expedition was his idea, and that Johnson had declined the command. Therefore, he would take charge.

Now the army had four commanders: Houston (who was claiming the army was being stolen from him), Fannin, Johnson, and Grant.

Bowing to the will of the council, on December 17 the governor ordered Houston to make a demonstration against Matamoros. Houston, who consistently valued Bowie as a leader of "promptitude and manliness," and rated him above other subordinates in "forecast, prudence and valor,"[7] promptly wrote him and ordered him to proceed to Matamoros and take the place. He reminded him that the port of Copano was important and also instructed him that "if any officers or men who have, at any time, been released on parole, should be taken in arms, they will be proper subjects for the consideration of court martial. Great caution is necessary in the country of the enemy."[8] Probably because Bowie was on the go so much, he did not receive the letter until much later.

In early January 1836, Bowie rode into San Felipe and asked the council to authorize him to recruit a regiment. Perhaps it was at this time that he asked them to give him a colonelcy. On January 12, the council turned him down, ruling that Bowie "was not an officer of the government nor army."[9]

When Johnson and Dr. Grant left San Antonio for Matamoros, Johnson had left Lieutenant Colonel Neill of the regular army in charge. Several days later, Houston received a courier from Neill with the unwelcome news that Johnson and Grant were on their way to Matamoros by way of Goliad, and in their haste to leave San Antonio the two men had stripped the garrison of all horses, blankets, provisions, and medicines. They had taken over two hundred officers and men with them, and had left behind only eighty sick and wounded.

Houston and his staff set out for Refugio and then went on to Goliad, where he caught up with some troops. He was in the middle of an impassioned speech to the troops, trying to persuade them to give up the foolish venture against Matamoros, when he was interrupted by a courier from Neill. The latter reported that two of his scouts had discovered that two of Santa Anna's generals had led separate troops across the Rio Grande in an invasion of Texas and were on their way to attack San Antonio. Santa Anna, with another large force of men, was following and would be in Texas shortly. Neill was calling for help to defend the Alamo, and he asked Houston for a furlough so he could visit his sick family.

Almost immediately Bowie rode up, asking for men to go back with him to defend the Alamo. Houston asked for volunteers to go with Bowie, and thirty responded. He then wrote out an order to Neill granting his furlough, but instructed him to remove all artillery from the Alamo and then blow it up "as it would be impossible to hold the town with the force there."[10]

Bowie and his thirty volunteers left Goliad on January 17, and arrived two days later in San Antonio.

CHAPTER 17

The Final Days: Siege of the Alamo

Antonio López de Santa Anna was born at Jalapa, Mexico, on February 21, 1794, of pure-blood Spanish parents. Enlisting in the Spanish Royal Army at the age of fifteen as a cadet, he did well in several engagements during Mexico's numerous revolutions. With his intelligence and talent for intrigue and changing sides at the right moment, he quickly won promotions, and by the age of twenty-eight he was a general. Santa Anna had great abilities and many faults, among which was an addiction to opium and pretty mistresses, preferably very young. Vain and capricious, he called himself "Protector of the People" and "the Napoleon of the West."[1]

Santa Anna hated all Anglo-Americans and was determined to crush the Texas revolt and expel all Anglos from the state. His pride had been severely wounded when Cos, his brother-in-law, had been defeated and forced to evacuate San Antonio. An order to his army had given instructions that all foreigners were to be treated as pirates and given no clemency. Now he was leading his army out of Mexico on his way to Texas to join his two generals and their divisions that were already there.

When Bowie and his force of about thirty men arrived at the Alamo, they found Neill and a force of 104 men. They had a few weapons and a few cannon, but were woefully short of supplies and powder, thanks to Johnson, Grant, and their confiscation tactics. Of the men under Neill's command, only nine were born in Texas, and they were Mexicans.

Bowie and Neill discussed Houston's instructions to blow up the fortifications. In his orders to Neill, Houston had given the latter some leeway and had instructed him to use his own judgment. Neill decided he didn't have enough oxen to move the artillery to a safe place, and decided against blowing up the fortress.

James Bowie, of course, was not a military man and knew little about military tactics or strategy. With the exception of Sam Houston (who had served under Gen. Andrew Jackson and for five years had been in the regular army as an officer) and a few others, the leaders in the Texas Revolution had very little military experience.

Bowie was an adventurer, a man of high intelligence, a splendid fighter, and a natural leader. At the same time, he was never a man to obey unquestionably orders from any man, even from his friend Houston. He didn't want to give up the fortress without a fight, and in this he was supported by the men. They were restless with inactivity and they, too, were spoiling for a fight. Taking this into consideration, Bowie concurred with Neill's decision.

On January 26, 1836, one of Bowie's men, James Bonham, organized a rally in support of Governor Smith. A resolution was passed in favor of holding the Alamo and demanding more supplies from the government, with the statement "we cannot be driven from the post of honor."[2]

As chairman of the meeting, Bonham was first to sign the resolution. The next signature was that of James Bowie. The men of the garrison had demanded $500 from the government, but knowing the mood of the general council, Bowie expected no help from that quarter. He personally negotiated a loan for the $500 and extended the scouting service, sending a detachment of young men as far as the Rio Frio.[3]

Due to his connections with the Veramendi family, his fluency in Spanish and his own ability to make friends, Bowie had great rapport with the predominantly Mexican population in San Antonio. A large number of these people consistently furnished him with information concerning the enemy's moves, and on January 22 he heard from the Navarro family that Santa Anna was marching on Texas with 4,500 troops. From the local padre he received news that the Mexican cavalry was heading for Bexar. Neill still had not gone home on his furlough, and for the time being the two were in joint command.

For some time Bowie had been physically ill, and it was only his determination that kept him going. Amos Pollard, the fort's surgeon, could not diagnose the illness, so called Dr. John Sutherland, a newcomer who had lately arrived with a contingent of troops from Alabama. Sutherland was also baffled, and could only say that the illness was "of a peculiar nature, not to be cured by an ordinary course of treatment."[4]

Bowie had set the men to work strengthening the defenses of the Alamo, but at night the restless men would spend their time in town, visiting the local cantinas and indulging in fandangos.

Señor José Cassiano was one of Bowie's Mexican friends who had volunteered for scout duty along the Rio Grande. On January 27 he galloped into camp with news that General Ramirez y Sesma was in Texas and there was no doubt that he was headed for San Antonio. Bowie promptly sent another courier off to San Felipe with the plea for "men, money, rifles, and cannon powder."[5] On February 2, another one of Bowie's contacts reported to him with the news that in addition to Sesma and his men, there were 5,000 more Mexicans following, and they too were headed for Bexar.

That same day Bowie wrote an impassioned letter to Governor Smith, asking for all possible help. In his letter he gave as his viewpoint "the salvation of Texas depends in great measure on keeping Bexar out of the hands of the enemy. It serves as the frontier picquet guard, and if it were in the possession of Santa Anna, there is no stronghold from which to repel him in his march toward the Sabine." As to the Alamo, he concluded: "Colonel Neill and myself have come to the solemn resolution that we will rather die in these ditches than give it up to the enemy."[6]

On February 3, Travis, who had been on recruiting duty by order of the governor, arrived in camp. Of his thirty troops, all except four were regulars. A few days later Davy Crockett, former congressman from Tennessee and a noted bear hunter, arrived with twelve other Tennesseans. Neill was still in command at the Alamo, but when he left San Antonio on February 17 to go on his furlough, he left Travis in command.

From the first there was friction between Bowie and Travis. Travis was a lieutenant colonel in the regular army, while Bowie was still a volunteer with no official rank in the army. Naturally, Travis contended he should be in command. Bowie, the best known fighting man in Texas and fourteen years older than the regular army officer, could not see himself taking orders from Travis and did not consider himself outranked as he was a colonel in the Rangers. When the decision was left to the men in the garrison, they elected Bowie as their commander with the rank of full colonel. This infuriated Travis more than ever, and there was still resentment on both sides.

Bowie was ill again with his mysterious ailment, and it was beginning to have a telling effect upon him. On the twelfth he went roaring drunk into town, claiming command of the entire garrison. He stopped private citizens from going about their business, and ordered town officials to open the calaboose and let everyone out. Then, when one of the freed prisoners, Antonio Fuentes, was thrown back into jail, Bowie exploded with rage. He called out his men from the Alamo and paraded them back and forth in the Main Plaza, about a mile from the Alamo. The men, all drunk, were shouting, cheering, and waving their rifles.[7]

Travis was disgusted with the whole situation and on February 13 wrote Governor Smith complaining about Bowie's drunken actions. He angrily wrote Smith that Bowie "was interfering with private property, releasing prisoners . . . & turning everything topsy turvy." He added that he was "unwilling to be responsible for the drunken irregularities of any man."[8] He stated that he would leave the place in an instant, but "it is more important to occupy this post than I imagined when I last saw you. It is the key to Texas."

In the interest of harmony, Bowie and Travis finally arranged a truce and on February 14, 1836, wrote the governor a letter concerning the situation and the way they resolved it. The solution was for Bowie to have command of the volunteers and for Travis to command the regulars and the volunteer cavalry, as that was the branch of service in which he had received his commission. Until Colonel Neill returned from his furlough, all general orders and correspondence would henceforth be signed by both men.

In any case, the quarrel became moot when on or about February 21 Bowie fell fifteen feet from a scaffold to the ground while attempting to mount a cannon for defense, crushing his ribs and breaking his hip.[9] This would only complicate his illness, which was variously described as tuberculosis, pneumonia, typhoid fever, typhoid-pneumonia, and "a disease of a peculiar nature." Whatever the illness, it rendered him helpless on his cot and confined him to his barracks room. During the time of Bowie's confinement to his cot he was nursed by a Mexican woman known as Madam Candelaria, who lived to be 100 years of age. For forty years she would be pensioned by the State of Texas until she died in January 1899.

Now that Bowie was unable to function properly, sole command of the Alamo passed to Travis.

On February 26, 1836, Davy Crockett made an entry in his journal that was found on him after the Alamo fell:

> Col. Bowie had been taken sick from over execution and exposure; he did not leave his bed until 12 o'clock. He is worth a dozen common men in a situation like ours — Col. Bowie's illness continues but he manages to crawl from his bed every day that his comrades may see him. His presence alone is a tower of strength.

Santa Anna was furious when he learned of the surrender of Cos in San Antonio and was determined to drive "those perfidious foreigners" out of Texas. With his treasury exhausted, he solicited funds from the Catholic church and borrowed money at high interest rates to finance his campaign. He started assembling his troops at San Luis Potosi, Mexico, in December 1835, and by the first week of February had reached Monclova. By this time his army numbered over 4,000 men with 1,800 pack mules, 33 large four-wheel wagons, and 200 ox-drawn carts. In addition there were a large number of sutlers (peddlers) and camp followers, mainly women.

The extremely cold weather in the dead of winter brought much suffering and death to the soldiers. At night the soldiers had to sleep on the cold ground, and food and water were scarce. There were no doctors to combat illnesses or ailments, no medicines and no ambulances, and no priests or chaplains to fulfill spiritual needs. Santa Anna's generals were plagued by desertions, inadequate care of their pack animals, illness, and transportation problems. Still, the dictator mercilessly drove his troops on.

When Santa Anna reached the Rio Grande on February 17, 1836, his generals urged him not to march to San Antonio as they considered that post insignificant and not worth taking. The dictator disregarded their advice. *El Presidente* was determined to have his revenge upon the Anglo upstarts for defeating his brother-in-law Cos. Incidentally, Cos had broken his parole not to enter Texas and engage in warfare and was now one of Santa Anna's commanders in the army.

Travis had been receiving frequent intelligence from Bowie's Mexican friends concerning the approaching Santa Anna and his generals, but was skeptical. Due to the harsh weather conditions, he and his fellow officers were doubtful the Mexican army would arrive before March. Sam Houston himself was of the same opinion.

The Mexican dictator surprised Travis by entering the outskirts of San Antonio on the morning of February 23. A sentinel in the tower of the Catholic Church of San Fernando had reported that the advance party of the enemy was in sight. Travis immediately sent out John W. Smith and Dr. John Sutherland on a scouting mission. They soon observed the Mexican forces behind Desiderio Hill and hurried back to Travis to make their report. Prior to the appearance of Santa Anna and his army, there was no regular commisariat at the Alamo. The men had scattered in squads over the city, getting food from where they could find it and sleeping when and where it suited their convenience. Every volunteer had a horse, but forage being unobtainable, these were kept in a herd on the Salado, five to six miles out of the city, where grass and water were abundant. The previous night the men had entertained themselves at a fandango. When they heard the report from the two scouts, Travis and the men promptly retreated into the Alamo and barricaded themselves in the fortress.

Thinking that Travis and his men had retreated to the mission Concepción, some two miles south of the Alamo, Santa Anna ordered Gen. Ventura Mora to take some troops and seize the mission. When one of his colonels, Juan Almonte, told him the mission, with its thick forty-five-inch limestone walls, would be a far more formidable fortress for Travis to defend than the Alamo, the Mexican commander was surprised that the Anglos chose to make their stand at the Alamo.

The original Alamo was a large compound originally used by Franciscan missionaries, and various quarters housed Indians whom the missionaries tried to convert. The convento, originally a two-story structure, contained the living quarters of the missionaries on the upper floor and offices, a guest house, dining room, and kitchen on the ground floor. A west wall was approximately 458 feet in length, while the south and north walls were approximately 161 feet. The east wall, which contained the convento and remained connected by a passageway to the former church, was approximately 190 feet long and 18 feet wide. It became the barracks — the Long Barrack, as they called it — of the Texas forces. The upper floor had been heavily damaged in the Battle of Bexar, and what remained was used as a hospital. The ground floor contained their armory and lodgings. The Long Barrack was chosen as the place where a final stand would be made, if necessary. James Bowie, when he became ill and then injured, was placed in a separate area known as the Low Barrack.

Today, of the original complex known as the Alamo, the Long Barrack and the former church baptistry are the only buildings still standing from the time of the famous battle.

With the entrance of His Excellency Santa Anna into Bexar, excitement among the citizens was high. Many Mexicans fled the city, while others stayed behind, hoping the dictator would win the war.

Capt. Almeron Dickinson of the Texas army took his wife, Susanna, and their infant daughter into the Alamo for safety. Other than the soldiers who remained to fight, Mrs. Dickinson and her daughter were the only Anglos in the fort. Both Bowie and Travis had their black slaves with them.

Bowie sent for fifteen-year-old Gertrudis Navarro and her married older sister, Juana Navarro Alsbury, and her eighteen-month-old son, Alijo. The two girls were cousins of his late wife Ursula, and were still residing in the Veramendi Palace.[10] Bowie called Juana to his side and said: "Sister, do not be afraid. I leave you with Colonel Travis, Colonel Crockett, and other friends.

They are gentlemen and will treat you kindly."[11] He then made sure that Juana, her child, and Gertrudis had a room separate from the other Mexicans who sought refuge in the fort.

James Butler Bonham was a native of South Carolina, and had just passed his twenty-ninth birthday during the siege of the Alamo. He had been a rebellious youth and something of a troublemaker. After three years at South Carolina College, his troublemaking activities caused him to be expelled. Notwithstanding this, he studied law, passed his bar examinations in 1830, and quickly built up a lucrative practice as he had a charming personality and was a natural leader.

Bored with his practice, Bonham had answered the call of his friend Travis to join him in Texas. First he helped recruit a contingent of young men known as the Alabama Grays, and reached San Antonio on December 12, 1835, just missing being able to participate in the Battle of San Antonio. Eight days later, he was officially commissioned a lieutenant of cavalry in the Texas army.[12]

Travis made much use of Bonham as a courier, and sent him to Goliad, where Col. James Fannin was entrenched with his army of some 450 men. In a message to Fannin, he described the situation at the Alamo and urged the colonel to come to his assistance with all of his men. Receiving no reply from Fannin, Travis sent off another courier by the name of Johnson with the same request. Signed by both Bowie and Travis, the message read:

> We have removed all our men into the Alamo, where we will make such resistance as is due to our honor, and that of the country, until we can get assistance from you, which we expect you to forward immediately. In this extremity, we hope you will send us all the men you can spare promptly. We have one hundred and forty-six men, who are determined never to retreat. We have but little provisions, but enough to serve us till you and your men arrive. We deem it unnecessary to repeat to a brave officer, who knows his duty, that we call on him for assistance.

Fannin still procrastinated.[13]

From the tower of the San Fernando church, the tallest building in San Antonio, Santa Anna had flown a long, flapping, blood-red banner, which could easily be seen from the Alamo. It was a sign that no quarter was to be given.

For a number of days there were no serious assaults on the Texans' barricade, since His Excellency was waiting for his heavy artillery to arrive, as well as for some more of his struggling units to catch up with him.

John McGregor served as second sergeant during the siege of the Alamo. A native of Scotland, he had lived in Nacogdoches before joining the army, and had fought at the Battle of San Antonio. Susanna Dickinson later gave interviews as to what happened during the shelling of the Alamo. She recalled how, during a lull in the siege, McGregor with his bagpipes and Crockett with his fiddle would entertain the troops with musical concerts and contests to boost the morale of the anxious men.

On February 23, Bowie, signing himself as commander of volunteers of Bejar, wrote a letter to Santa Anna:

> Because a shot was fired from a cannon of this fort at the time a red flag was raised over the tower, and soon afterward having been informed that your forces would parley, the same not having been understood before the mentioned discharge of cannon, I wish to know if, in effect, you have called for a parley, and with this object dispatch my second aide, Benito James, under the protection of a white flag, which I trust will be respected by you and your forces. God and Texas.

The Mexican commander had his aide, Col. José Batres, answer for him. Santa Anna refused to parley and made it clear that the rebellious foreigners had no recourse except to immediately place themselves at the disposal of the Supreme Government.[14]

At 9:00 on the morning of February 24, 1836, the siege of the Alamo began in earnest. Santa Anna ordered a frontal advance on the fort and commenced firing a battery of two eight-pounders and a howitzer. Two hours later, he ordered the firing stopped and with his cavalry reconnoitered the vicinity. Later that day, Travis sent a courier through the lines with a letter to Governor Smith. It was addressed "To the People of Texas & all Americans in the world" and declared he was opposed by a thousand or more Mexicans under Santa Anna. The letter stated the enemy demanded surrender or the garrison was to be put to the sword, but that he would never surrender or retreat. Travis asked that help be sent him since the enemy was constantly receiving reinforcements and should have an army of three or four thousand in a few days. He concluded with the ringing words: *"Victory or Death."* A postscript was added, in which he revealed the men had found eighty or ninety bushels of corn in deserted stores, and had managed to get into the walls twenty or thirty head of beeves.

On March 1, 1836, fifty-eight delegates assembled in Washington-on-the-Brazos, a hamlet that consisted of about a dozen cabins, or shanties, and with stumps still standing in what passed for a street. The delegates settled down to business in a crude shelter, an unfinished structure with cloth instead of glass in the windows. The building was owned by a gunsmith and part-time preacher named Noah Ayres.

The purpose of the delegates was to organize a convention, set up a government, and declare complete independence from Mexico. They did this the following day. Three days later, Sam Houston, who was a delegate, was elected "Commander-in-Chief of all the land forces of the Texian army, both regulars, volunteers and militia . . . and endowed with all the rights, privileges and powers due to a Commander-in-Chief in the United States of America." There was only one dissenting vote.

The convention was called to order in a special session on Sunday, March 6, while Richard Ellis, the president of the convention, read another appeal from Travis. It had been written three days earlier and had just arrived.

Once more Travis was calling for help. His requests for aid from Fannin had fallen on deaf ears, and now the enemy was bombarding very heavily from a distance of 400 yards. In addition, they had been encircling the Alamo with entrenched encampments on all sides. Seeking reinforcements, on February 25 Travis had sent a plea to the town of Gonzales. Capt. Juan Seguin had been chosen as courier. That evening he rode out of the Alamo on James Bowie's fast horse and managed to bluff his way past a Mexican patrol as he galloped to Gonzales.[15] Thirty-two men responded to the urgent plea of Travis, and managed to make their way into the fort. Santa Anna, Travis now estimated, had a force of from 1,500 to 6,000 men, and he believed another 1,000 men had just arrived to assist the Mexican general.

Eventually, Fannin started moving his troops toward San Antonio to assist Travis, but his wagons were heavily overloaded and broke down within a few hundred yards from Goliad. He then promptly retreated back into his Fort Defiance.

The delegates to the convention in Washington-on-the-Brazos didn't know it, but when Richard Ellis read the emotional letter from Travis, the doomed Alamo had fallen. Santa Anna, with his vast superiority in manpower and material, had finally made his assault upon the Texan stronghold.

CHAPTER 18

Aftermath

When the carnage was over, Santa Anna entered the Alamo. Incredible as it may seem, some seven men had survived the bloody battle. Among them was the famous Davy Crockett, who had been in Texas barely a month.

Gen. Manuel Fernandez Castrillon had the men brought before the dictator and tried to intervene for them. Santa Anna then severely reprimanded Castrillon for not having them killed on the spot, and personally ordered their execution. Some of the sapper officers fell upon the victims with savage ferocity and killed them, horribly mutilating them in the process. Santa Anna then ordered the 188 bodies of the Texans stripped, subjected to brutal indignities, and then thrown into heaps and burned. After viewing the bodies, Santa Anna greeted Capt. Fernando Urizza and commented: "It was but a small affair."

Francisco Antonio Ruiz was the scion of a prominent Mexican family and was *alcalde* of San Antonio when Santa Anna arrived in February 1836. Ruiz remained loyal to the Texas cause and was placed under house arrest by the Mexican army. According to Ruiz, Santa Anna ordered him to bury the Mexican dead — whom he estimated at some 1,600 — and to confirm the identities of Travis, Bowie, and Crockett. He also helped in collecting the bodies of the dead Texans and placing them on the funeral pyre, the number totaling 182.[1]

There were several other survivors of the Alamo, including Mrs. Susanna Dickinson and Angelina, her fifteen-month-old daughter, and Joe, a black body servant of Travis. Joe had been ordered by the Mexican dictator to point out the bodies of his master Travis, and of Bowie. In addition, survivors included Gertrudis Navarro and her sister, Mrs. Juana Alsbury, and Juana's young son, Alijo.

When Mrs. Alsbury was released from the Alamo she met Manuel Perez, the brother of her first husband. Still dazed at what she had been through the past several days, she failed to recognize him. "Sister," he cried, discovering Juana standing in the debris, "don't you recognize your own brother-in-law?"[2]

Others who survived the ordeal were Señora Ana Esparza and her four children: Enrique, Francisco, Manuel, and Maria de Jesus. The *señora*'s husband, Gregorio, had been one of the defenders of the Alamo and had been killed in the fighting. Then there were Trinidad Saucedo and Petra Gonzales. José Maria Guerro survived and escaped death by convincing the Mexican soldiers that he was a prisoner of the Texans. Also surviving was Henry Warnell, who died later from wounds received in the battle.[3]

Apparently Bowie's black slave died with him in the Alamo, as on a list of names of those killed in the fortress, prepared by the Daughters of the Republic of Texas, there is listed "John, a negro."

As the victorious troops stormed the breastworks and walls of the venerable building and ran through the rooms, killing the defenders, sometimes in hand-to-hand combat, these survivors huddled in fear wherever they were. Later, when Bowie's mother was informed of his death at the Alamo, she calmly remarked: "I'll wager no wounds were found in his back."[4]

The Battle of the Alamo happened more than a century and a half ago. One man among the defenders, Louis Moses Rose, was not among the combatants who fought in the battle. Before the storming of the Alamo, Rose climbed over the wall and managed to escape the watchful eye of the sentries and patrols as he made his way to safety.

It is those few survivors who brought to the world our knowledge of what happened within the walls of the fortress before the Mexican troops made their final assault. There are always doubters, and there are those who have questioned the validity of certain reported incidents.

Did Travis actually draw his famous line in the dirt, explaining to the men that their cause was doomed and there was no escape? And did Col. James Bowie ask that his cot be carried across the line? Rose told this story to many people over the years, but first to A. P. Zuber, who lived on Lake Creek in what is now Grimes County. Rose had known Zuber since 1827, and headed for his home after using his fluent Spanish to move through the Mexican lines. According to him, Bowie remarked to him: "You seem not to be willing to die with us, Rose."

"No," answered Rose, "I am not prepared to die and shall not do so if I can avoid it."

Rose claimed that the line-drawing incident, and Bowie being carried across the line in his cot, was also witnessed by Mrs. Dickinson, Travis' black servant Joe, and Enrique Esparza.[5] Young Esparza later gave his account of the battle, and related how his father, Gregorio, had died. After the battle, Gregorio's brother Francisco, who sided with Santa Anna, recovered his brother's body and had it buried in the Campo Santo cemetery. Gregorio Esparza was the only one of the defenders to receive a Christian burial.

As John King Beretta wrote in the *Southwestern Historical Quarterly* in 1939: "Is there definite proof that Travis did NOT draw the line? . . . If not, then let us believe it."

There is another question that has aroused considerable controversy. Did Davy Crockett actually die during the battle or did he surrender, along with several others, to be executed on direct orders of Santa Anna?

For years Crockett has been revered as an authentic Texas hero, and his exploits as shown on a popular television series some years ago have made his name a household word to our nation. Could this noteworthy man, known for his quick wit and his laughter, a former congressman and noted bear fighter, expert with a rifle, have possibly surrendered instead of dying by an opponent's bullet, bayonet thrust, or sword?

To the consternation of many true believers, the facts do seem to bear out that Davy—along with five or six other men— did surrender instead of going down fighting.

Col. José Enrique de la Pena was a staff officer with Santa Anna on his expedition into Texas, and was with him at the storming of the Alamo. He kept a diary of his experiences during that period. For many years the diary was suppressed, but a translation by Carmen Perry was finally published by Texas A&M University Press in 1975.

In the diary, de la Pena plainly states that Crockett and his fellow men were either captured alive or surrendered, and then on orders of Santa Anna died as previously dexribed. At least six other Mexican soldiers who were in the battle support de la Pena's testimony.

A century and a half after the death of Bowie, the manner of his death remains in controversy. According to Alcalde Ruiz, Bowie was found "dead in his bed" in a side room.[6]

In 1838, Dr. John Sutherland, who had been one of the scouts at the Alamo, related he saw on a wall, near the spot where Bowie's cot had been, marks made by the splattering of Bowie's brains. Dr. Sutherland had it both from Travis' slave Joe and Mrs. Dickinson that several rifle balls went through Bowie's head while he lay unable to lift it from his pillow.

Gertrudis Navarro, one of the female survivors, told Mrs. Samuel Maverick only two years after the fall of the Alamo that she saw Mexican soldiers enter Bowie's room, to which she and other women had fled, and bayonet him. They then carried him, still breathing, upon their bayonets into the plaza. Another report is that Bowie, unable to rise and fight, shot himself.[7]

A Mexican officer wrote that Bowie died "like a woman almost hidden under a mattress." W. P. Zuber related that a fifer in Santa Anna's band told that while soldiers were gathering the bodies of the slain for burning, four brought Bowie, still alive, on the cot to their captain. The captain reviled him as a traitor to his country and his dead wife. Bowie retorted "in excellent Castillian" with such acidity that the captain ordered four soldiers to spread-eagle him and a fifth to cut out his tongue. Then he had him cast alive on the raging fire.

It is generally believed that Bowie died in his cot, back braced against the wall, and using his pistols and famous knife. It is certainly easy to believe that Bowie, the renowned fighting man, took some Mexican soldiers to the grave with him.

And what happened to the remains of those gallant defenders who gave their lives at the Alamo in defense of freedom? What happened to their remains after the torches were set to their funeral pyres?

Their ashes and bones were found in at least three places, all within a few hundred yards from the Alamo.[8] On February 25, 1837—almost a year to the day after the final assault began—then Col. Juan Seguin, who had rendered notable service as a scout and courier for both Travis and General Houston, paid honors of war to the remains of those who perished at the Alamo. The heaps of remains were carefully collected and placed in a coffin with the names of Bowie, Travis, and Crockett engraved inside the lid. A procession slowly led the way to the Cathedral of San Fernando, where the ashes rest in peace and dignity today.[9]

In the final analysis, what difference does it make if Travis did or did not draw a line, or if Bowie did or did not have his cot carried across that line? What difference does it make if Crockett and a few others died in battle, were captured alive, or surrendered and were executed? They all died fighting for a young nation in being and a cause in which they all fervently believed. Regardless of how they died, they did so honorably and are rightfully heroes of Texas.

Although Bowie was supposedly a wealthy man, an appraisal of his estate showed little of value. An inventory of his belongings revealed the following:

> A Masonic apron of lambskin, valued at $4.00.
> A pair of "crape" pants, 50 cents.
> A blue cloth coat, 13 cents.
> Blue cloth jacket, 25 cents.
> Black cloth dress [presumably Ursula's] $2.00.
> A cotton hunting dress, $1.50.
> Pair of blue cloth pants, 12 cents.
> A "casonet" vest, 25 cents.
> Woman's apron, 25 cents.
> Pocket wallet, 6 cents.
> 2 pocketbooks at $1.00.
> Trunk at 25 cents.
> "Whipsaw" at $6.00.
> One cross cut saw at $4.00.
> 2 mill saws at $2.00.
> 640 acres of land.

At auction, the total realized from the above was only $99.50.[10]

The present Governor's Palace in San Antonio, used by the old Spanish governors before Mexico became a republic, is said to have James Bowie's desk on display there.

What happened to the horse and saddle Bowie owned when he entered the Alamo? According to legend, it was given to James Bonham to use as a courier to bring help to the besieged fortress. His portrait, painted in New Orleans, had long since been given to one of his Louisiana relatives and was not part of his estate. As recently as November 1991, various members of the Bowie family were contesting in a New Orleans court the ownership of a portrait of the famous knife fighter credited to renowned nineteenth-century artist George Peter Alexander Healy. Measuring about two by three feet, the painting depicts a determined young Bowie gripping the handle of a sword-knife.

For years after Bowie's death, his heirs fought over his estate. Ursula Bowie's grandmother, Josefa Ruiz Navarro, was the inheritor of the whole Veramendi estate. She died in 1837 and left other Navarros to inherit and make claims against the Bowie estate.

Eugenio Navarro stated that a coach in Monclova belonging to James Bowie had been sold for $800 and the money credited to his account with the Veramendi business firm.

Adolphus Sterne lived in Nacogdoches and had been a strong supporter of the Texas Revolution. In his diary of February 15, 1839, he wrote that in January of that year, according to the *National Banner*, the treasurer of the Republic of Texas paid to the estate of James Bowie the following sums: $33.66; $100.00; $100.00; and $137.40, totaling $371.06. These were payments for services Bowie rendered during the late war.

There were many administrators of the Bowie estate, and as late as 1900 Martha Bowie Burns, daughter of Bowie's brother John, showed up with a lawyer. The two contended Martha was the sole survivor of all of James Bowie's brothers, and was the rightful heir to the section of land that had in 1840 been sold by order of the San Jacinto probate court. It had been patented in La Salle County in 1860 and had been resold several times. The 1900 owner considered it cheaper to pay Martha Bowie Burns, and her attorney, $160 to quiet his title than to fight the case through court.[11]

And what became of the Veramendi Palace after the death of Don Juan Martin Veramendi and his family? This building was originally built in the 1740s, and the 400-foot frontage mansion was purchased by Governor Veramendi's father on February 5, 1780, for the then monetary equivalent of $1,880. The building stood on the east side of Soledad Street, between present-day Commerce and Houston streets. When Veramendi's father died, Don Juan Martin inherited the home. After the death of the family and James Bowie, the Veramendi Palace for a number of years served as a hotel. It subsequently became a curio shop and a saloon, and was torn down in 1909 when Soledad was widened. Today, the high, scarred doors of the Veramendi Palace are on display in the Alamo.

The vice-governor owned considerable land. On March 15, 1845, a deed was signed by Prince Solms and by Rafael Garza and his wife, Maria Antonia Veramendi, selling 16,000 acres near New Braunfels that had belonged to Ursula's father.

On May 4, 1924, the *Houston Chronicle* published an article entitled "The Romance and Tragedy of Veramendi Palace." This article stated that due to Vice-governor Juan Veramendi's great sympathy with the cause of the Texas colonists, he was ordered by the Mexican authorities to report to the Mexican capital in Mexico City. He was ordered to take his entire family, including Ursula and a child, with him. Once in the capital he was removed from his office of vice-governor. The *Dallas Morning News* on December 2, 1928, carried a similar story stating that Veramendi was forced to return to Mexico and was removed from office. Both articles state that Bowie, at this time, was away from home and had no knowledge of what transpired until he returned to the Veramendi Palace.

This, of course, contradicts the story that Bowie urged his wife to go to Monclova to avoid the cholera epidemic then raging.

If Veramendi was recalled to Mexico City in disgrace and removed from office, he must have been quickly reinstated. Microfilm records at the Center for American History at the University of Texas at Austin show that Veramendi in the summer of 1833, and as late as August, was writing various letters to Bexar pertaining to government business. In one letter, dated August 3, the vice-governor approved medical expenses for citizens of Goliad.

Some factions are of the belief that James and Ursula never had children. Their belief usually hinges on these facts: that James never mentioned his children in his will; that although the parish records of San Fernando Church in San Antonio show the baptism and marriage of Bowie to Ursula, there are no records existing showing any baptism or christening of any Bowie children; and that the Monclova priest, José Francisco Soberon, when listing the names of those he buried in September 1833, and the dates of their death due to the cholera epidemic, failed to mention any Bowie children. The padre, however, listed the senior Veramendis, Ursula, and Santiago Veramendi, an adopted son of Don Juan Veramendi. Other members of the family listed were José Suarez, who was married to Josefa Veramendi, and Maria Veramendi, widow of Tomás Valdez.

On September 26, 1833, José Antonio Navarro, brother of Josefa Veramendi, wife of the vice-governor, wrote his friend Samuel Williams concerning the death of his sister and her family. In his sorrow he mentions that "Bowie no longer has a wife," but nothing at all is said concerning any children.

To refute the story that the Bowies had no children, both the *Houston Chronicle* of May 4, 1924, and the *Dallas Morning News* of December 2, 1928, state that James and Ursula had a daughter. The *Chronicle* claims that on March 20, 1832, a daughter, Marie Elve was born. The *News* mentions a daughter, but gave her name as only Marie.

Perhaps both children were born in Monclova, and that might be the reason the San Fernando church has no record of any baptisms. Monclova, Mexico, is about 300 miles from San Antonio, and in those days of travel by carriage a journey was exceedingly slow. As Ursula was pregnant when she and her parents left for Monclova to avoid the cholera epidemic that later claimed her life and that of her family, it is possible she gave birth to a second child somewhere along a lonely road, or in some small village without a doctor or a priest to baptize the child. Hence, no birth records—especially if the child died shortly after birth.

This, of course, conflicts with the records of the International Genealogical Index of the Church of Jesus Christ of Latter-Day Saints that state a son, James, was born to her on July 18, 1833, in Monclova, Coahuila. The records of the church also show that

Maria Josepha Elve Bowie, a daughter, was born to her on April 18, 1832, and not March 20, as the *Chronicle* claims. The place of birth, or baptism, was given as the Villa De San Fernando De Bejar. As San Antonio was highly affected by the cholera epidemic at that time, it is suggested that perhaps the priest or priests of San Fernando Cathedral moved out of the city to avoid the cholera, and perhaps the records got lost during that period of troubled times.

Caiaphas K. Ham knew Bowie very well as an intimate friend and companion in arms. He stated that Bowie and Ursula had two children. And there was Enrique Esparza who, as a young lad, had been rescued by James after falling into a river. His father, Gregorio, had been one of the defenders of the Alamo, and Enrique, his mother, and other family members had been in the Alamo during the siege. As an old man he had been interviewed by the *San Antonio Daily Express,* and the May 12, 1907, edition carried his memories of what transpired in the Alamo while it was under siege. He recalled the incident of being saved by Bowie, and remarked that the latter had been a lonely man after his wife and two children had died.

One's family should certainly know if one has children. In an interview published in *DeBow's Southern and Western Review* of October 1852, Bowie's older brother John remarked that James and Ursula had one child. John's daughter, by then Mrs. M. A. Burns, stated the Bowies had one daughter, who died of cholera. And both John S. Moore and Mrs. Eugene Sonniat, grandchildren of Rezin, claim the Bowies had two children.

Lucy Leigh Bowie, a relative of James, gave the world much pertinent information about her famous relative in the paper she prepared that was read at the meeting of the Bucks County Historical Society held in Doylestown, Pennsylvania, on June 17, 1916. In this paper she emphatically denied the authenticity of the information supposedly given by John J. Bowie to a Dr. Kilpatrick of Temple, Louisiana, in the October 1852 edition of *DeBow's Southern and Western Review*:

> ... the article in De Bows Review is absolutely false. I have carefully gone over it several times item by item and every statement I find untrue. It purports to come from John J. Bowie whose family papers I have now before me, and they coincide with those in the possession of the rest of the family connection,

and bear no trace of such statements as made in De Bows Review.
It is probable that John J. Bowie never knew of that article.

Years after his death, James Bowie was still entangled in controversy.

So ends the saga of James Bowie — frontiersman, fighting man, husband, father, worthy friend, and patriot.

Notes

Prologue

1. There are various estimates as to how many people were killed at the Alamo, generally ranging from 183 to 189. The figure of 188 is taken from a list of names of the dead, prepared by the Daughters of the Republic of Texas.

2. Virgil E. Baugh, *Rendezvous at the Alamo*, 97.

3. "The Alamo Long Barrack," compiled by the Daughters of the Republic of Texas, 41. This event was witnessed by several people, including Mrs. Susanna Dickinson, widow of one of the defenders; Joe, Travis' black body servant; Enrique Esparza, who was present as the son of one of the Mexicans who fought with the Texans, and Louis Rose himself. They all subsequently told their stories to several interviewers.

4. Richard G. Santos, *Santa Anna's Campaign Against Texas*, 35. The infantry's equipment was predominantly British; English flintlock rifles firing a one-and-a-half-ounce ball, ramrods, flints, locks, bayonets, steel saber and scabbards, and even British brass drums. The alternate rifle was a British Baker flint ignition gun weighing nine and half pounds without bayonet, three feet, nine and a half inches in length, with a thirty-inch barrel of .615 caliber firing a 350 grain bullet at 1,200 feet per second, with sighting to 200 yards.

5. John Myers Myers, *The Alamo*, 225. Account of Mrs. Susanna Dickinson.

Chapter 1

1. Amelia Williams, "A Critical Study of the Siege of the Alamo and of the Personnel of Its Defenders," *Southwestern Historical Quarterly* 37, no. 2 (October 1933): 90.

2. Walter Worthington Bowie, *The Bowies and their Kindred.*

3. *Ibid.*, 259, 260.

4. *Ibid.*, Introduction.

5. *Franklin Sun*, Winnsboro, Louisiana, August 16, 1956.

6. Walter Worthington Bowie, 260, 261.

7. John Henry Brown, *Encyclopedia of the New West*, 433.

8. James Bowie's place of birth has been given variously as Burke County,

Georgia; Elliott Springs, Tennessee; and Logan County, Kentucky, with various dates being given as 1790, 1795, and 1796. Bowie's brother John, who was considerably older than he was, in an interview about the Bowie family in *DeBow's Review* (October 1852) stated that James was born in Logan County, Kentucky, in 1796.

9. Baugh, *Rendezvous at the Alamo*, 17.

10. John J. Bowie, in an article in *DeBow's Review*, 13 (July–December, 1852) entitled "Early Life in the Southwest — The Bowies," 378.

11. Raymond W. Thorp, *Bowie Knife*, 119.

12. *De Bow's Review*, 13: 378, 379.

13. *Ibid.*, 379.

14. Walter Worthington Bowie, 261, 262.

Chapter 2

1. *DeBow's Review*, 13: 379, 380.

2. *Ibid.*

3. Letter dated July 27, 1984, from William R. Williamson to Charles Long, curator of the Alamo.

4. Raymond W. Thorp, *Bowie Knife*, 121.

5. In an anniversary edition of the Opelousas, La., *Daily World* of June 1970, an article on page 59 states: "The marriage of James Rezin Bowie was recorded in Marriage Record Book No. 1, page 256, of the St. Landry Catholic Church on Sept. 15, 1814 . . . he signed the book James Rezin Bowie."

6. John Myers Myers, *The Alamo*, 101.

7. Virgil Baugh, *Rendezvous at the Alamo*, 22, and *Niles National Register* 56 (July 20, 1839): 324, 325.

8. Baugh, 23.

9. J. Frank Dobie, *Heroes of Texas*, 35.

10. *DeBow's Review*, 13: 380.

11. Amelia Williams, "A Critical Study . . . ," 103.

12. *DeBow's Review*, 378.

13. *Ibid.*

14. Noah Smithwick, *The Evolution of a State*, 138.

15. *The Daily Intelligencer* of Doylestown, Pennsylvania, of June 20, 1916, in an article prepared by Lucy Leigh Bowie and read at the meeting of the Bucks County Historical Society held in Doylestown, June 17, 1916.

16. *Ibid.*

17. Elve Bowie died at the home of her son-in-law, Alexander Sterrett, at Shreveport, Louisiana, in 1837. She was a real pioneer woman, and was noted throughout the Southwest for her kind nature and fine principles. Alexander Sterrett married Martha Bowie, whose first husband, James Nugent, was killed in an accident. Sterrett was the first sheriff at Shreveport and was killed in the performance of his sheriff's duties.

18. John Henry Brown, *Encyclopedia of the New West*, 436, 437.

Chapter 3

1. Herbert Asbury, *French Quarter*, 158.

2. Lyle Saxon, *Lafitte The Pirate,* 15.
3. Asbury, 159.
4. *Ibid.,* 161.
5. Saxon, 146.
6. *Ibid.,* 156.
7. Asbury, 167.

Chapter 4

1. Henderson Yoakum, *History of Texas,* I: 196.
2. J. Frank Dobie, *Heroes of Texas,* 36.
3. Mitchell V. Charnley, *Jean Lafitte, Gentleman Smuggler,* 185.
4. Horace H. Shelton, "Under Texas Skies."
5. Claude Leroy Douglas, *James Bowie: The Life of a Bravo,* 45.
6. *DeBow's Review,* 13: 378.
7. Clifford Hopewell, *Sam Houston: Man of Destiny,* 140.
8. Beginning around 1780, for more than forty years these octaroon balls were held in New Orleans. At these balls white men and the women of mixed blood danced, and many of these quadroons and octaroons were beautiful and became mistresses of the white men. Children born to them were baptized and their records were kept in the Catholic church.
9. *DeBow's Review,* 13: 381.
10. Amelia Williams, "A Critical Study . . . ," 91.
11. Raymond W. Thorp, *Bowie Knife,* 82.
12. Dobie, *Heroes of Texas,* 45.
13. *Ibid.,* 37.

Chapter 5

1. J. Frank Dobie, *Heroes of Texas,* 37.
2. *DeBow's Review,* 13: 381.
3. John Lyde Wilson. *The Code of Honor; or Rules for Government of Principals and Seconds in Duelling;* Charleston, T. J. Eccles, 1838.
4. Clifford Hopewell, *Sam Houston,* 47, 48.
5. *Funk & Wagnalls Standard Reference Encyclopedia,* 4414.
6. Hopewell, 48.
7. Raymond W. Thorp, *Bowie Knife,* 12.
8. *Ibid.,* 14.
9. *Ibid.*
10. From an article written September 1, 1830, by Willie Williamson, a friend of Bowie, while he was in New Orleans. Also, W. W. Bowie's *The Bowies and Their Kindred,* 273, 274.
11. Both a statement by Dr. Maddox and Colonel Crain's letter specify the big knife that Bowie used during the fight.

Chapter 6

1. *Galveston Daily News,* March 31, 1890.
2. *Southwestern Review* 16, no. 3 (April 1931): 355–356.

3. *Ibid.*, 356.

4. *DeBow's Review* 13 (October 1852): 381.

5. J. Frank Dobie, "Bowie and the Bowie Knife," *Southwest Review* 16 (April 1931): 356.

6. Andrew J. Sowell, *Rangers and Pioneers of Texas*, 126–127.

7. Horace H. Shelton, "Under Texas Skies," 30.

8. Dobie, "Bowie and the Bowie Knife," 355.

9. Amelia Williams, "A Critical Study . . . ," 94.

10. William R. Williamson, "A Case For Bowie," *The American Blade*, Nov/Dec 1980: 16, 17.

Chapter 7

1. Raymond W. Thorp, *Bowie Knife*, 16.

2. *Ibid.*

3. *Arkansas Gazette*, July 9, 1828.

4. Hempstead County Probate Court Records, October 25, 1841.

5. Thorp, 21.

6. *Ibid.*, 22.

7. *Ibid.*, 23.

8. Williamson, "The James Black Legend," *The American Blade*, Jan/Feb 1978: 21.

9. Thorp, 28.

Chapter 8

1. Hempstead County Circuit Court Records, July 18, 1828.

2. *Ibid.*, June 1, 1829.

3. *Ibid.*, October 3, 1870.

Chapter 9

1. Raymond W. Thorp, *Bowie Knife*, 36.

2. *Ibid.*, 37.

3. Doylestown *Daily Intelligencer*, June 20, 1916.

4. Noah Smithwick, *The Evolution of a State*, 136–137.

5. William R. Williamson, "Daniel Searles of Baton Rouge," in *Arms Gazette*, January 1975: 21.

6. Thorp, 90.

7. Williamson, "Daniel Searles of Baton Rouge," 18.

8. Thorp, 89.

9. Williamson, "Rezin Bowie's Personal Knife," in *Arms Gazette*, December 1973: 22.

Chapter 10

1. Bowie, in *The Daily Intelligencer*, Doylestown, Pennsylvania, June 20, 1916.

2. Clifford Hopewell, *Sam Houston: Man of Destiny*, 141.

3. Conveyance Records, Assumption Parish, Napoleonville, Louisiana.

4. Virgil Baugh, *Rendezvous at the Alamo*, 36.

5. Conveyance Records, Lafourche Parish, Louisiana.
6. Thomas McKinney to Stephen F. Austin, February 13, 1830. Austin Papers 2:331.
7. *De Bow's Review*, 13: 381.
8. Hopewell, 229.
9. S. Rhodes Fisher to Stephen F. Austin, August 14, 1830. Austin Papers 2: 465.
10. Eugene C. Barker, *Life of Stephen F. Austin*, 165–166.
11. Walter Prescott Webb, *The Texas Rangers, A Century of Frontier Defense*, 20.
12. Amos A. Parker, *Trip to the West and Texas, 1834-35*.
13. Horace H. Shelton, "Under Texas Skies," 27.
14. *The Daily Intelligencer*, Doylestown, Pennsylvania, June 20, 1916.
15. Letters from Edmund Bowie, Temple Hills, MD, to the author, October 2 and November 10, 1989.
16. *Ibid.*

Chapter 11

1. Jean Flynn, *Jim Bowie, A Texas Legend*, 34.
2. Certified translation copied from the originals, Fontaine Papers, University of Texas Archives, by R. S. Buguor.
3. *Fort Worth Press*, October 16, 1963.
4. Howard R. Driggs and Sarah S. King, *Rise of the Lone Star*, 156, 157.
5. J. Frank Dobie, *Heroes of Texas*, 40.
6. *Ibid.*
7. *Ibid.*, 40, 46.
8. Walter W. Bowie, *The Bowies and Their Kindred*, 270; *San Antonio Express*, May 21, 1905. This paper gives the reminiscences of Mrs. Francis Gelhorne, whose father was a tavern keeper at Gonzales. Bowie and his wife frequently stopped at her father's house, and she described "Ursulita" as a woman beautiful in person and character.
9. Horace H. Shelton, "Under Texas Skies," 28.
10. John Henry Brown, *Indian Wars and Pioneers of Texas*, 137.
11. Shelton, 35.
12. The house was originally built in the 1700s and, Spanish-style, was one-story high with the rooms forming a hollow square and opening out on a veranda bordering a patio, where flowers and shrubs lent the privacy to its occupants (*Houston Chronicle*, May 4, 1924.) After the death of the Veramendi family, the dwelling eventually became a museum and was finally torn down in 1909. (*San Antonio News*, November 17, 1965.) Two huge doors of the home are on display in the Alamo.
This Veramendi Palace, or Governor's Palace as it was also known, is not to be confused with the adobe Spanish Governor's Palace, which still stands on the northwest corner of Military Plaza in San Antonio. This building is the governor's residence where Moses Austin presented to Spanish officials his case for colonization.
13. Dobie, 41. His footnote 18 says: "In 1869 there was a lawsuit filed in Colorado over Bowie's headright league of land on the Navidad River. The

lawsuit, styled M. A. Veramendi et al vs. W. J. Hutchins et al, furnished details of how Bowie lived with the Veramendis."

    14. Walter Lord, *A Time To Stand,* 28.

    15. Flynn, 38, 39. The International Genealogical Index of the Church of Jesus Christ of Latter-Day Saints (Mormons) states the daughter was born April 18, 1832, and the son was born July 18, 1833.

    16. J. A. Quintero, "The San Saba Gold and Silver Mines," *Texas Almanac* for 1868, 33–35.

    17. Driggs and King, 165.

    18. Baugh, 68.

    19. Article reprinted by the *Frontier Times,* 27 (October 1949): 14, 15.

    20. Dobie, 51.

    21. *Ibid.,* 40.

    22. A typewritten copy of this letter, translated into English, is filed with the Nacogdoches Archives, Archives Division, Texas State Library, 83: 112, 113.

Chapter 12

    1. *De Bow's Review,* 380.

    2. Martha Ann Turner, *William Barrett Travis, His Sword and His Pen,* 17.

    3. *American Notes and Queries,* July 27, 1889, 155.

    4. Raymond W. Thorp, *Bowie Knife,* 113.

    5. Walter Lord, *A Time To Stand,* 27.

    6. Noah Smithwick, *Evolution of a State,* 198.

    7. George McAlister, *A Time To Love . . . A Time To Die,* 53.

    8. *Ibid.,* 53.

    9. Thorp, 131, 132.

    10. Juan N. Seguin to W. W. Fontaine, April 10, 1874. Fontaine Papers, University of Texas at Austin.

    11. Amelia Williams, "A Critical Study . . . ," 99.

    12. John Henry Brown, *Indian Wars,* 136.

    13. John J. Linn, *Reminiscences of Fifty Years in Texas,* 303.

    14. *San Antonio Light,* May 4, 1917.

    15. John Henry Brown, *Encyclopedia of the West,* 436, 437.

    16. Howard R. Driggs and Sarah S. King, *Rise of the Lone Star,* 216.

    17. Brown, *Encyclopedia,* 436, 437.

    18. Linn, 302–304.

Chapter 13

    1. Emerson Hough, *The Story of the Outlaw,* 38, 39.

    2. Raymond W. Thorp, *Bowie Knife,* 129.

    3. *Galveston Daily News,* March 6, 1889.

    4. Thorp, 23.

    5. John Henry Brown, *Encyclopedia of the New West,* 438.

    6. John Myers Myers, *The Alamo,* 99, 100.

    7. Virgil Baugh, *Rendezvous at the Alamo,* 61.

    8. Walter W. Bowie, *The Bowies and Their Kindred,* 275.

    9. Ben C. Truman, *The Field of Honor,* 290–294.

10. Baugh, 60.
11. *San Antonio Light,* May 4, 1917.
12. Baugh, 62.

Chapter 14

1. *Daily Intelligencer,* Doylestown, Pennsylvania, June 20, 1916.
2. Henderson Yoakum, *History of Texas,* 1: 290.
3. *Texas Gazette,* January 10, 1832.
4. Clifford Hopewell, *Sam Houston,* 145.
5. Yoakum, 1: 298.
6. *Ibid.*
7. Letter dated September 26, 1833, from Bexar to Samuel Williams from Jose Antonio Navarro, brother to Josepha Veramendi.
8. *Dallas Morning News,* January 7, 1895.
9. J. Frank Dobie, *Heroes of Texas,* 41. Due to the death of the entire Veramendi family, Ursula's grandmother, a Navarro, inherited the Veramendi estate.
10. Harriet Smither (ed.), "Adolphus Sterne's Diary," *Southwestern Historical Quarterly,* 30: 306.
11. Hopewell, 163.
12. General Land Office of Texas, Vol. 30.
13. Dobie, *Heroes of Texas,* 42.
14. James Bowie to James B. Miller, June 22, 1835. Texas State Archives, Austin.
15. The papers of Mirabeau Buonaparte Lamar, 5: 358.
16. John Forbes to James B. Miller, July 24, 1835. Domestic Correspondence, Texas State Archives.
17. Hopewell, 163.
18. James Bowie to Henry Rueg, August 2, 1835, Nacogdoches Archives (MS), Texas State Archives.

Chapter 15

1. Clifford Hopewell, *Sam Houston,* 140.
2. *Ibid.,* 166.
3. Anna J. H. Pennybacker, *A New History of Texas for Schools.*
4. Donald Day and Harry Herbert Ullum (eds.), *The Autobiography of Sam Houston,* 14.
5. Austin's Army Orders, Texas State Archives.
6. *Ibid.*
7. James Bowie's report to Austin.
8. Minutes of Council of War, and Austin to Bowie and Fannin, November 2, 1835. Army Papers, Texas State Archives, Houston to Fannin, November 13, 1835.
9. Letter in files of the Alamo Museum.
10. John Henry Brown, *History of Texas, 1685-1892,* 1: 372.
11. *Texas State Historical Association Quarterly* 2, no. 1: 34.
12. Yoakum, 2: 18.

Chapter 16

1. As reported by Lt. Gov. Robinson, in John Henry Brown's *Indian Wars and Pioneers of Texas*, 136.

2. Stephen F. Austin's Order Book for 1835. *Texas State Historical Association Quarterly* 2, no. 1: 54.

3. Hobart Huson, *Captain Phillip Dimmitt's Commandancy of Goliad*, 22.

4. When the battle was over, Milam's body was buried where he fell and he was given a Masonic burial. The DeZavala Chapter of the Daughters of the Texas Revolution later moved his body to Milam Park in San Antonio, and a monument was erected to his memory. (*Houston Chronicle*, May 4, 1924.)

5. Walter Lord, *A Time To Stand*, 57.

6. Wallace O. Chariton, *100 Days in Texas*.

7. Dobie, *Heroes of Texas*, 43.

8. Amelia W. Williams and Eugen Barker (eds.), *Writings of Sam Houston*, 1: 323.

9. W. Roy Smith, "The Quarrel between Governor Smith and the Council of the Provisional Government of the Republic," *Texas State Historical Association Quarterly*, 5: 327.

10. Henderson Yoakum, *History of Texas*, 2: 58. Order to James Bowie, January 17, 1836.

Chapter 17

1. Clifford Hopewell, *Sam Houston*, 144.

2. David Nevin, *The Texans*, 90.

3. Walter Lord, *A Time To Stand*, 78.

4. *Ibid.*

5. *Ibid.*

6. *Ibid.*, 79.

7. *Ibid.*, 85.

8. Nevin, 90.

9. John J. Linn, *Reminiscences of Fifty Years in Texas*, 134.

10. The girls were nieces of Col. José Antonio Navarro, brother of Mrs. Juan Martin Veramendi. Vice-governor Veramendi had married the sister of the girls' father and had adopted Juana. Her first husband had died, and she had married a Dr. Alsbury.

11. Lord, 106.

12. Ben Proctor, in *Heroes of Texas*, 21–27.

13. Lord, 98, 99.

14. Amelia Williams, "A Critical Study of the Siege of the Alamo and of the personnel of its Defenders," *Southwestern Historical Quarterly* 37, no. 1 (July 1933).

15. Nevin, 101.

Chapter 18

1. "The Alamo Long Barrack Museum," 11, 42. However, a list of the dead compiled by the Daughters of the Republic of Texas shows 188 dead.

2. Walter Lord, *A Time To Stand,* 176.
3. *Ibid.*
4. Dobie, *Heroes of Texas,* 35.
5. "The Alamo Long Barrack Museum," 41.
6. Dobie, *Heroes of Texas,* 45.
7. *Ibid.*
8. "The Alamo Long Barrack Museum," 43.
9. *Ibid.*
10. *San Antonio Express,* May 10, 1918.
11. Dobie, *Heroes of Texas,* 47.

James Bowie Monument. Bowie County is named for the hero.

Bibliography

Books

Adair, Garland, and M. H. Crockett, eds. *Heroes of the Alamo.* New York: Exposition Press, 1957.

Asbury, Herbert. *French Quarter.* New York: Alfred A. Knopf, 1936.

Barker, Eugene C. *Life of Stephen F. Austin.* Dallas: Cokesbury Press, 1925.

———. *Mexico and Texas 1821-1835.* New York: Russell & Russell, Inc., 1965.

Batson, James L. *James Bowie and the Sandbar Fight.* Madison, AL: Batson Engineering & Metalworks, 1992.

Baugh, Virgil E. *Rendezvous at the Alamo.* New York: Pageant Press, 1960.

Binkley, William. *The Texas Revolution.* Baton Rouge: Louisiana State Press, 1952.

Bowie, Walter Worthington. *The Bowies and Their Kindred.* Washington, DC: Cromwell Bros., 1899.

Brown, John Henry. *History of Texas.* 2 vols. St. Louis: L. E. Daniell, 1892.

———. *The Encyclopedia of the New West.* Marshall, TX: 1881.

Chariton, Wallace O. *100 Days in Texas.* The Alamo Letters. Plano: Wordware Publishing, Inc., 1989.

Dobie, J. Frank, et al. *Heroes of Texas.* Waco: Texian Press, 1964.

Douglas, Claude Leroy. *James Bowie: The Life of a Bravo.* Dallas: Banks Upshaw and Company, 1944.

Driggs, Howard R., and Sarah S. King. *Rise of the Lone Star.* New York: Frederick A. Stokes Company, 1936.

Fehrenbach, T. R. *Lone Star: A History of Texas and the Texans.* New York: American Legacy Press, 1983.

Field, Dr. Joseph E. *Three Years in Texas.* Greenfield, MA: Justin Jones, 1836. Reprinted by The Steck Company, Austin: 1935.

Flynn, Jean. *Jim Bowie, A Texas Legend.* Austin: Eakin Press, 1980.

Foote, Henry Stuart. *Texas and the Texans.* 2 vols. Austin: The Steck Company, 1935.

Frantz, Joe Bertram. *Texas: A Bicentennial History.* New York: W. W. Norton & Company, Inc., 1976.

Gambrell, Herbert, and Virginia Gambrell. *A Pictorial History of Texas.* New York: E. P. Dutton & Co., Inc., 1960.

Hopewell, Clifford. *Sam Houston: Man of Destiny.* Austin: Eakin Press, 1987.

Hough, Emerson. *The Story of the Outlaw.* New York: The Outing Publishing Co., 1907.

Houston, Andrew Jackson. *Texas Independence.* Houston: Anson Jones Press, 1938.

Linn, John J. *Reminiscences of Fifty Years in Texas.* Austin: State House Press, 1968.

Lord, Walter. *A Time To Stand.* New York: Harper & Brothers, 1961.

McAlister, George A. *A Time To Love . . . A Time To Die.* San Antonio: Docutex, 1988.

——. *Alamo: The Price of Freedom.* San Antonio: Docutex, 1988.

Myers, John Myers. *The Alamo.* Lincoln: University of Nebraska Press, 1948.

Nevin, David. *The Texans.* The Old West Series. New York: Time-Life Books, 1975.

Parker, Amos A. *Trip to the West and Texas, 1834–35.* Concord, NH: White and Fisher, 1835.

Pennybacker, Anna J. H. *A New History of Texas for Schools.* Tyler, TX: Published by the author, 1881.

Pope, William F. *Early Days in Arkansas.* Little Rock: Frederick W. Alsopp, 1895.

Santos, Richard G. *Santa Anna's Campaign Against Texas.* Waco: Texian Press, 1968.

Saxon, Lyle. *Lafitte The Pirate.* New Orleans: Robert L. Crager & Company, 1950.

Smither, Harriet, ed. *The Papers of Mirabeau Buonaparte Lamar.* 6 vols. Austin: Von Boeckmann-Jones Co., 1920–1927.

Smithwick, Noah. *The Evolution of a State.* Austin: The Steck Company, 1935.

Sowell, Andrew J. *Early Settlers and Indian Fighters of Southwest Texas.* Austin: 1900.

——. *Rangers and Pioneers of Texas.* San Antonio: Shepard Brothers and Co., 1884.

Thorp, Raymond W. *Bowie Knife.* Albuquerque: University of New Mexico Press, 1848.

Tinkle, Lon. *13 Days To Glory.* College Station: Texas A&M Press, 1958.

Truman, Ben C. *The Field of Honor.* New York: Fords, Howard and Hulbert, 1884.

Turner, Martha Anne. *William Barret Travis, His Sword and His Pen.* Waco: Texian Press, 1972.

Webb, Walter Prescott, ed., et al. *The Handbook of Texas.* 2 vols. Austin: Texas State Historical Association, 1952.

——. *The Texas Rangers, A Century of Frontier Defense.* Austin: University of Texas Press, 1935.

Wellman, Paul T. *The Iron Mistress.* New York: Doubleday & Company, Inc., 1951.

Williams, Amelia W., and Eugene C. Barker, eds. *The Writings of Sam Houston, 1813–1863.* 8 vols. Austin: University of Texas Press, 1938–1943.

Wortham, Louis J. *A History of Texas.* 5 vols. Fort Worth: Wortham-Molyneaux Company, 1924.

Yoakum, Henderson. *History of Texas, From Its First Settlement in 1685 to Its Annexation to the United States in 1846.* 2 vols. New York: J. S. Redfield, 1885.

Articles

Barker, Eugene C. "Land Speculation as a Cause of the Texas Revolution." Texas State Historical Association *Quarterly* 10.

Bowie, John J. "Early Life in the Southwest — The Bowies." *DeBow's Review,* July–December 1852.

Dobie, J. Frank. "Bowie and the Bowie Knife." *Southwest Review* 16, (April 1931).

Quintero, J. A. "The San Saba Gold and Silver Mines." *The Texas Almanac,* 1868.

Smith, W. Roy. "The Quarrel between Governor Smith and the Council of the Provisional Government of the Republic." Texas State Historical Association *Quarterly* 5, no. 1 (July 1901).

Williams, Amelia. "A Critical Study of the Siege of the Alamo and of the Personnel of Its Defenders." *Southwestern Historical Quarterly* 37, no. 1 (July 1933) and no. 2 (October 1933).

Williamson, William R. "Rezin Bowie's Personal Knife." *Arms Gazette,* December 1973.

——. "Daniel Searles of Baton Rouge." *Arms Gazette,* January 1975.

——. "A Case For Bowie." *The American Blade,* November/December, 1980.

——. "The James Black Legend." *The American Blade,* January/February 1978.

Booklets and Pamphlets

"The Alamo." Long Barrack Museum. Compiled by the Daughters of the Republic of Texas, 1986.

Shelton, Horace H. "Under Texas Skies." Texas Heritage Foundation 2, no. 6 (November 1951).

Letters

Bowie, Edmund, Temple Hills, MD, to Clifford Hopewell, October 2 and November 10, 1989.
Fisher, S. Rhodes, to Stephen F. Austin, August 14, 1830.

Microfilm Records

Roll No. 158, Center for American History, University of Texas at Austin.

Newspapers

Arkansas Gazette, July 9, 1828.
Dallas Morning News, January 7, 1895; December 2, 1928.
Doylestown *Daily Intelligencer,* June 20, 1916.
Fort Worth Press, October 13, 1963.
Franklin Sun, Winnsboro, Louisiana, August 16, 1956.
Galveston Daily News, March 6, 1889; March 31, 1890.
Houston Chronicle, May 4, 1924.
Houston Post, February 16, 1936.
Opelousas *Daily World,* June 1970.
San Antonio Express, May 10, 1918; April 22, 1934; February 2, 1969.
San Antonio Light, May 4, 1917; July 9, 1930.
San Antonio News, November 17, 1965.
Texas Gazette, January 10, 1832.

Public Documents

Austin's Army Orders, Texas State Archives, Vol. 11, no. 1.
Conveyance Records, Assumption Parish, Napoleonville, Louisiana.
Conveyance Records, Lafourche Parish, Louisiana.
Hempstead County Circuit Court Records, July 18, 1828; June 1, 1829; October 3, 1870.
Hempstead County Probate Court Records, October 25, 1841.
Minutes of Council of War, and Austin to Bowie and Fannin, November 2, 1835. Army Papers, Texas State Archives.
Stephen F. Austin's Order Book for 1835. Published in Texas State Historical Association *Quarterly* 2, no. 1.

Index

9 781940 130194